"Conversation at Pilings" by the noted Maine artist Michael Palmer. Ink and acrylic on canvas: 36"x48": 1973: Collection of the author.

MAINE
IN TRANSITION

For Robert Beardsley
Best wishes –
Betty Joyce

MAINE
IN TRANSITION

Writings from the York County Coast Star

1961 – 1973

By

Betty Joyce

Published with the Sponsorship of

The Maine Historical Society

by

PHOENIX PUBLISHING

West Kennebunk, Maine

All the stories included in this volume were originally published in the *York County Coast Star* and are copyrighted. They are reprinted here with minor modifications in some cases by special permission of the *York County Coast Star* which reserves all rights.

Library of Congress C.I.P. Data

Joyce, Betty, 1911-
Maine in transition : writings from the York County coast star, 1961-1973 / by Betty Joyce.
p. cm.
Includes index.
ISBN 0-914659-56-1 : $25.00
1. York County (Me.) – Social life and customs – Anecdotes. I. Maine Historical Society. II Title.
F27.Y6J69 1992
974.1'95043 – dc20 92-63
CIP

Maine in Transition
Writings from the York County Coast Star / 1961–1973

Printed in the United States of America

To Marg,

Morty, and Ruth,

who opened, each,

a door

CONTENTS

INTRODUCTION

THE PARTNERSHIP of journalism and regional history has been a long and fruitful one. From the *Falmouth Gazette,* Maine's first newspaper published in 1786, to today, local feature stories have preserved and celebrated Maine's community lore and traditions. Historians know how to bring to such accounts an awareness of context and intent, separating fact from fiction. Yet often newspaper features have been the only venue for publishing local history. As such, they are of great importance to the scholar and casual reader alike.

Betty Joyce's *Maine in Transition: Writings from the York County Coast Star* is an excellent example of this partnership. Her choice of subjects demonstrates an enthusiastic engagement in community life a generation ago, offering an enjoyable blend of memory, history, and journalism.

The time period covered by these articles – the 1960s and 1970s – is a past so near that we may resist considering it "historical." But for Maine, these were pivotal decades. Transportation and communication changes as well as education reforms strengthened links with the world beyond Maine's borders. More aggressive marketing of tourism created a romanticized image of life in Maine, often at odds with economic reality. The beginnings of in-migration by people "from away" brought new attitudes and expectations, transforming community institutions. In the eclectic yet comprehensive array of articles presented in *Maine in Transition,* the reader will find evidence of these social, cultural, and demographic shifts. Betty Joyce provides an armchair tour of York County twenty-five years ago.

Rich layers of heritage are honored by articles on historic houses and museums. Continuing a pattern established along coastal Maine one hundred years earlier, Maine's dramatic landscape and image of a simple life lured a new generation of artists and craftspeople. But other articles presage public policy controversies of the 1990s: concern about the quality of the environment and apprehension about nuclear energy plants. Ultimately, the articles demonstrate what has been and will always be of value in community history. It is the stories of people's lives, the daily ebb and flow, the involvement with family and town, the accounts of the personal and public experiences we share.

The Maine Historical Society is delighted to sponsor *Maine in Transition* and we commend Betty Joyce and Phoenix Publishing for undertaking this project. By gathering and updating these articles in a single volume, they have provided us with an excellent opportunity to discover and reflect upon an important chapter in Maine history. Our intent in sponsoring *Maine in Transition* is to acknowledge the valuable partnership of journalism and regional history and encourage amateur historians and scholars to turn their investigative energies to Maine's recent past.

Elizabeth J. Miller
Executive Director
Maine Historical Society

December 20, 1991

FOREWORD

The visitor to the attic knows the risk he runs when he lifts the lid from a box of old letters. Words out of the past have a power to detain. Hours later he may find himself still crouched on the floor, savoring the pain and embarrassments of an early love, and with leg cramps to boot.

Foreword from
The Points of My Compass
by E. B. White

CHANGE A FEW words—"cellar" for attic, "clippings" for letters, "occupation" for love—and the first paragraph of my foreword, although a bit pilfered, is done. The rest is more difficult. First, there are too many thank-yous for adequate expression to those who helped with galleys and page proofs: Louisa Hall, Lucinda Lord, Barbara Mitchell, Mary Whiteside. And to Polly Day, Eddie Cote, Joy Earhart, and the Nguyen Family who saw to it that I ate properly when I'd forget to look at the clock, and to friends who gave moral support.

Special gratitude goes to Alexander (Sandy) Brook "without whom this book, etc. . . . " The *York County Coast Star* used to be a spindly little weekly called the *Kennebunk Star* at the time in the fifties when a young Sandy traveled north to buy it and become its editor. He inherited the printers, got an associate and a receptionist/stenographer and was in business. It wasn't too long before the *Star*, as it was and still is called, began to expand. When more help was needed a middle-aged woman applied and Sandy showed his mettle by hiring her—she who knew nothing about journalism except how to spell it.

The woman was I, and I learned the craft the easy way, by osmosis. Three of us staff members occupied a little room in the small, derelict building that housed the *Star* (see "Cushioning Future Shock", page 202). We all heard each other's phone calls and answers, shared failures and triumphs, likes and dislikes. Only once do I remember being "taught" (no doubt there were others) when I wanted large type for a head on news I'd brought in. "You'd use type that large," Sandy told me, "only when Wells declares war on Ogunquit." I learned too that even editors, highly elevated as captains of ships, have frustrations seldom pandered to because of tradition. Sandy disliked the editorial "we." Writing an editorial that mentioned his wife Anneke, he was heard to say "Damn! I can't say *our* wife!"

His humor was probably what kept him his sanity as the *Star* gradually encompassed coastal towns from the Kennebunks to the New Hampshire border and changed its name to the *York County Coast Star.* Never, as far as I know, did he change his convictions about values born in our antecedents and passed on in their children. Sandy wrote about them, and sorrowfully about those of us now who would denude forests; build on open spaces that once offered views and the fragrance of flowers; despoil our water, our earth, our air. He spoke out forcefully against the growing trend toward destruction of what Nature had intended for all living things to enjoy and be sustained by.

Lest all this sound like an obituary, Sandy is alive and well, retired, and lives out of state. But the *Star*'s story deserves a book of its own and those of us who took even a small part in the fun and anxieties of its growing pains hope it will be written by the one who was its editor before, during, and after the period covered here.

Regrettably it was not possible to recheck all of the information contained in the final section, "Towns." Since these articles were written, so many changes have occurred that it was felt best to leave the text essentially as originally written. For any resulting sins of commission or omission concerning historical facts, I apologize.

The fact is this book is not what I intended it to be, a booklet of stories selected from the *Star* from a personal file I'd kept in my cellar while reporting for the paper. The booklet was to be a kind of memento — small but in hard cover — for friends and relatives. It would occupy me during those "golden years" that too often become tarnished if not kept alive.

Phoenix, however, had a different viewpoint. My stories, they said, represented a period of transition in Maine. My book, they urged, should contain only what fit that concept. It would, in short, be a history book.

A history book! This alarmed me. I'd been force-fed the usual history books of my time (those endless dates to memorize!) from grade one on up. History was Columbus, the pyramids, Ivan the Terrible – people and places and actions benign and malignant that at some time had been considered eligible for permanent recording. No, I told Phoenix. History books were the job of aged pundits. Aged I was, pundit, no. I ended the argument with a softer version of: No way is my book to be presented as history.

Phoenix won. I came to realize that the parameters of history have no boundaries, except that of the future. History occurred yesterday and when tomorrow comes today becomes history, and changes in our lives take place as we draw in breath and exhale it. The lesson may be that the values and ways of life we hold today should be scrutinized, with their effect on the future in mind, as minutely as a scientist examines what he sees through his microscope.

So here it is, *Maine in Transition,* a history book.

Betty Joyce

Kennebunk, Maine
January 16, 1992

MAINE
IN TRANSITION

1

Towns

The Goat Island lighthouse off Cape Porpoise, smallest on the coast of Maine / Photo by Nancy Ames, 1991

Cape Porpoise

June 24, 1965

WHEN YOU LONG for tranquility, take a ride a few miles north of Kennebunkport to Cape Porpoise. Now a quiet retreat from the pleasure-bent resort areas around it, Cape Porpoise was once the busiest town on the Maine coast, boasting the largest harbor between Portsmouth and the Saco River. It was the beginning of our coastal settlements, a community of fishermen that later added farming to its activities and by 1641 had a healthy trade with the West Indies.

Sadly it is often the bad that is recorded, the good being taken for granted, and we learn from early records that the Cape was a place of turbulence, with the people of Saco bringing charges of drunkenness and other vices against "those rogues who came out of the rocks of Cape Porpoise." Like most of the early settlements it was feeling its way toward law and order, but it took an earthquake to prod the scared inhabitants into building a church. Its first minister was a Harvard graduate, a schoolmaster, a competent blacksmith and an excellent fisherman — a range of activities that few ministers can boast of today.

On the tip of the Cape, on a slight rise, there's a plaque telling of an incident during the Revolution. In August of 1782 a British ship lay off the coast. It had captured a schooner and a sloop and was preparing to use its guns on the community. It was at this moment that one Samuel Wildes, infuriated at the capture of the schooner, jumped into a dory and rowed out to the side of the enemy ship demanding that the schooner be released. "Leave immediately," he ordered the Britishers.

The marines roared with laughter and ordered him aboard, whereupon Samuel turned about and headed for shore. The Britishers aimed their guns at him and shot and wounded him. This was more than the men of Cape Porpoise, watching on shore, could bear. They assembled under the leadership of Lt. James Burnham on Goat Island — and in fury put the British ship to rout with their muskets. It was a short but decisive battle. The Cape men lost their leader and the Britishers counted seventeen dead. These were buried beyond the harbor as the enemy ship put out to sea.

A Cape Porpoise superstition has it that on the battle's anniversary weird lights mark the spot where the seaman's bones lie, and that Cape fishermen returning with their catch on that day can sometimes hear, as if from far away, the faint sound of taps.

Sea-sprayed Cape Porpoise started out as Porkpisces (Latin: porcus-hog, pisces-fish). The Cape went through a lot of spelling changes—Porpisces, Porpisse, Porpesse, Porpess, and you'll still see "Cape Porpus" signs hereabouts. Nineteen years after the town was incorporated in 1653, it appeared in the county records as Cape Porpoise.

You may even see a porpoise, the "sailor's friend," playing off Cape shores. They're called that because porpoises, it is said, have been known to guide shipwrecked sailors to safety, laying never a harmful fin on them en route.

Now the Cape does not even dream of its turbulent past. The fishing boats put out at dawn and drift home in a lowering sun with their catch, fish of all kinds that you will eat that same night in restaurants dotting the Maine coast. Not much prettier a sight can be seen, from one of the Cape's own quaint restaurants, than Goat Island's tiny lighthouse, the smallest on the coast of Maine, at the entrance to the outer harbor; and nearby a small pink structure that glows garnet in the last rays of the sun.

Biddeford

June 29, 1966

WHILE SACO SLEEPS her beauty sleep across the river, her twin sister, Biddeford, bustles. Once Biddeford was quiet and beautiful too. Colonial homes and stately elms lined her streets. Stage coaches brought visitors from Boston and farther south for enjoyment of the gracious hospitality this Maine coastal city offered.

Then one day, around 1825, a Boston syndicate harnessed the falls of the river and a cotton mill was born. One by one more industries grew up, and one by one the lovely homes were torn down to make way for "progress."

Back in their beginnings, Biddeford and Saco were one and included Old Orchard. They were known as Winter Harbor Plantation and remained so until 1653 when Maine was absorbed by Massachusetts. Then Winter Harbor became Pepperellborough (changed in time, understandably, back to Saco) on the east side of the river, and on the west Biddeford, named for Bideford ("by-the-ford") in England.

History tells us terror reigned in the early days. "The whole country was in arms. Men went to their business bearing their muskets, and women worked with well-charged muskets beside them. In the fields one farmer worked while another guarded the spot. At public worship the laymen literally watched while the clergy prayed; armed men sat at the ends of the seats for the protection of the women."

You may walk the streets of Biddeford today with no more fear than what might be caused by an occasional wayward vehicle. And while you may decry the loss of her beautiful homes, you will probably be relieved to find this commercial hub near at hand to answer your shopping needs.

Kennebunk

July 20, 1966

KENNEBUNK, "the only village in the world so named," thus claimed a sign that graced the old Kesslen shoe factory (now the home of gift shops, a bank, offices of lawyers, etc.) by the falls that powered it.

Kennebunkers give thanks all the time though for things they have that people come from other places to see. They're honest about them too. As far as we know, no one in Kennebunk ever claimed Washington slept there. But General Lafayette did — in the home, still standing, of Revolutionary officer Col. Joseph Storer. Lafayette in his strolls around his old friend's property no doubt rested his eyes on a young elm tree, an elm you can see today—ancient now, doomed now by Dutch Elm disease, after decades of spreading wide its leafy branches like some rich, tropical growth.

Take a drive through the streets of Kennebunk. See those numerals over many doors or on corners of houses; "1787," "1802," "1790," and so on. They are not just numbers, they are dates. And behind each of the narrow-clapboarded facades are lovingly cared-for heirlooms, wide polished floor boards, old fireplaces brought into the light of day in most cases from behind half a century of boards. In at least one of these homes a smoke room still retains a whiff of the smoked meats that once hung from the great hooks.

Sayward Street ends on the banks of the Mousam where Kennebunk's first sawmill stood. It was built in 1672 by Henry Sayward, called the "Father of Kennebunk."

Another sawmill nearby, where Bartlett's Bridge is now on Route 1, was operated by the Littlefields (*sic*). But in ten years the mills and their families had disappeared, victims of Indian tomahawk, arrow, and fire. It was almost fifty years before any more enterprise was attempted in Kennebunk.

Near what is now Durrell's Bridge at The Landing in Kennebunk there occurred in 1726 one of the great tragedies of those early times. Philip Durrell returned from the fields one day to find his wife and son, his married daughter and her baby, vanished and his house in ashes. When the Indians had taken them the women had time only to scoop up the family bible. It was dropped in their hurried flight and discovered the next spring, its leaves sodden with winter snows, its cover warped. But it was all Philip Durrell had left of his wife and children. Painstakingly he removed the pages from the binding, drying each one separately, and had the book rebound. He married again and the book has passed down through generations to its present owner, Mrs. E. Stanley Brown of Kennebunkport, who treasures it under glass.

See the bell in the steeple of the Unitarian Church on Main Street. You'll have to climb a ladder to touch it but not every day do you touch something Paul Revere made. And the pulpit in the church was made from a single log of mahogony found adrift in the Gulf of Mexico.

Here is a place of ancient things and ancient houses. Stay and dream awhile in the land of your fathers.

Cape Neddick

August 10, 1966

THE HISTORY of Cape Neddick can be traced to 1602 when an English navigator, Gosnold, his ship at anchor, looked toward its forbidding cliffs and rocky shores. He deliberated over the sketches of the coast drawn for him on the deck by friendly Indians — and sailed away, but not before giving the name "Savage Rock" to what is now the Nubble.

Cape Neddick used to be one of the liveliest spots on the Maine Coast. That was in the days when it was a stopover for the stagecoaches that made their journey twice a week between Portland and Boston. "Marm Freeman" kept her tavern there in the 1800s. A tavern was the hub of the community then. The mail was dropped off there, distinguished wayfarers often stopped overnight, and local folk gathered at taverns for fun and games. Longfellow was one notable who used to stay at Marm Freeman's tavern on his way to and from his Portland and Cambridge homes.

In our New England beginnings, Cape Neddick had no clearly defined boundaries. A few fishermen may have built temporary shelters there, but the area was a no-man's land sandwiched between Ogunquit (then called Wells) and York. In 1652 it appeared on a map, now in the British museum, showing four houses belonging to the "Gooches, Weares, Wheelwrights, and Stovers" — names you will still see and hear around the Cape today.

Residents and summer visitors turn their eyes seaward countless times a day, and stare at a man-made thing of beauty. It is Nubble Light, a white exclamation point almost at the end of a long paragraph of scenic wonder that is the coastline of Maine from Eastport to Kittery.

Take the drive around Cape Neddick some evening just after sunset. Park your car at Nubble light and watch its yellow rays sweeping the waters below. Make sure it's a clear, warm summer night and you'll be richly rewarded. Do it soon before the fog starts rolling in and the chill of fall winds once again blunt the sharpness of its beam.

The Cape Neddick Light Station, more familiarly known as Nubble Light / Photo by the author, 1966

The Yorks

August 17, 1966

THE YORKS—York Beach, Harbor and Village—are places of "firsts and onlies."

The first English settlement on York soil was founded in 1631 by Edward Godfrey of England, York's first colonist. York Village was the first "city" to be incorporated in America, in 1641. On Point Christian, the early name for Gorges Point, was the Governor's Palace, the first and only feudal manor in Maine.

Off the York mainland is Boon Island, a bleak, rocky mound that saw Maine's only known cannibalism. In December, 1710, the "Nottingham Galley" bound from London to Portsmouth crashed on the island, stranding those aboard for almost a month. Those who lived, in order to stay alive, ate those who died.

The trial of the first person in Maine to receive the death penalty was held in York. Goody Cornish was executed in 1645 for murdering her husband. There wasn't much proof, but judgment was on the basis of the "bleeding of the dead body whenever she came near it."

When the wife of Reverend Bachiler was convicted of adultery in 1651, the letter "A" was branded on her cheek. She carried it on her face to her grave, the only known instance of such a penalty in Maine. (The record of her trial and sentence is supposed to have given Hawthorne his idea for *The Scarlet Letter.*)

Kittery

August 24, 1966

"OLD KETTERIE" was the only part of New England that George Washington saw on his tour of New England in 1789. "On my way to the mouth of the harbor," goes his diary (put into modern spelling), "I stopped at a place called Kittery in the Province of Maine. From thence I went by the old Fort on an island which stands at the entrance of the harbor, and where the lighthouse stands. As we passed this we were saluted by 31 guns. Having lines we proceeded to the Fishing Bank . . . and fished for Cod, but its not being a proper time of tide we hit only two . . . "

Explorers stepped on Kittery's shores as far back as 1614. It was then that the Newi Indian village chief built his wigwam at what is now South Berwick. Probably the first white settler was an Alexander Shapleigh who had come from a section called Kittery Point in the town of Kingsweare, Devonshire, England. After him came others, whose beautiful houses, built in the seventeenth and eighteenth centuries, can still be seen in Kittery and Eliot. These men gave names like Dumpling Hill, Dearing's Guzzle, Lover's Lane, Slut's Corner, Tripe's Corner to Kittery, names now forgotten. But one, Cow Cove, is still in use and marks the place where the *Pied Cow* tied up, a ship that once brought supplies, including a hogshead of malt for "beare," to colonizers from England.

It was in Kittery's shipyard that the *Ranger* was built, under the supervision of Captain John Paul Jones. The *Ranger* was the first ship built in America to be saluted by a foreign power. Kittery was also the birthplace of Sir William Pepperell. Besides having all sorts of places and things named after him (including a brand of sheets) he was the only man born in an American colony to be given a British baronetcy.

George Washington truly slept in Kittery, but it is doubtful that he visited the widow of Sir William since that lady, now a widow and an embittered Tory, rejected Washington as president and claimed loyalty only to King George III. Our first president must nevertheless have enjoyed his stay in Kittery, some of whose lovely homes still exist. In fact,

Spruce Creek at Kittery Point, winter / Photo by Armsden, 1966

if Washington were to arise from his grave and come back he would find less change than in any of the colonies he visited in his many travels.

Back in the early 1600s what we now know as Kittery was "Newichawannock," an Indian village. Later many of the Indians died in an epidemic, and when the colonists moved in they encountered little opposition to their appropriation of the Indians' land.

Probably Kittery was named after Kittery Point, a section of a small town in Devonshire, England. But some like to think it was named for a pretty girl, Kitty Rye, who lived in the Fort McClary area.

However it was named, in "old Ketterie" you will find much still standing that housed the life of our earliest colonists.

Biddeford Pool

June 21, 1967

IN 1616 CAPTAIN Richard Vines was sent from England to the northeast corner of the new world (what is now Maine) by Sir Fernando Gorges to test its climate for colonization. Vines and his company anchored in a natural harbor which he named Winter Harbor, now called Biddeford Pool.

The men built log cabins and in spite of Maine's well known winter cold apparently had a healthy winter. The records state that "not one of them felt their heads to ache while they stayed there," although an epidemic (no doubt brought over in the ship) raged among the neighboring Indians.

After the first winter, Vines began transporting settlers from England, and a fishing community was formed on the shores of the little harbor. He himself began procuring more and more land until he finally owned all the lands within the present boundaries of Biddeford. He may have overextended himself because eventually he disposed of his vast holdings for only about $500 and left for the West Indies in 1645 where he died soon after.

His departure marked the decline of the colony he had helped found. It never again regained its former glory as a fishing and trading center, but the day came when city dwellers discovered this wildly beautiful part of Maine's coast, which was still within easy distance of shops and entertainment, and the summer resort of Biddeford Pool was born.

Drive your car north to "The Pool" from Kennebunkport along Route 9. Watch the surf crashing in great geysers on stormy days or creaming in over the black rocks on quiet ones. See the Pool's mansions. And think back a mere three hundred years to when a little band of men braved a long winter's gales to found the first colony.

Ogunquit

July 26, 1967

THINK OF OGUNQUIT as it used to be, the few large estates, scattered shingled cottages, the huddle of fishing shacks at the Cove, later a few hotels. Think of that when you are trying to find a parking place in Ogunquit today.

And speaking of the Cove, it was only about eighty years ago that the river mouth was redirected to Perkins Cove from the "Mouth of the River Cove." Ogunquit in fact might be another town from the one described in old records: " . . . the little fishing village spliced to the skirts of Wells where the road winds across the rocky wastes . . . that in some places you almost double on your own footsteps."

Its transformation from a small fishing village to an art colony and vacation paradise has placed Ogunquit among the top resorts of the world. One of its attractions though, its beach, was once in danger of passing forever out of the control of Ogunquit citizens. In 1888, three miles of land skirting the Atlantic waters here was bought for $300 by the state. When the rich and the artists, flocking to this picturesque part

Ogunquit harbor / Photo by the author, 1967

of the coast, tried to buy shore property, the fact was revealed that it had been sold by the state to a man from New Hampshire who, moreover, was planning in turn to sell it to outside interests. The beach was saved by the residents, who formed a corporate village and after a long period of litigation bought the land back for $45,000.

In the 1800s artists began a stepped-up migration. They found the small village of Ogunquit and its surroundings inspirational, some even claiming that nowhere else could they find the special atmospheric conditions that seemed to give lustre to their canvases. Artist Charles Woodbury, coming somewhat later and finding even up into the early 1900s only the houses of the natives, the fishing shacks and one hotel, started an art school that brought students flocking to the area. Today Ogunquit as an art center, with its museum and numerous galleries, has no peer along the whole New England coast.

Still later, about forty-five years ago (1922), a summer theatre was begun by Walter Hartwig, an associate of David Belasco. The Ogunquit Playhouse is now run by John Lane who brings to it each summer the Broadway successes that delight his audiences; and they may even see one or two tryouts that won't reach Broadway until fall.

In spite of its change from a simple fishing village to one of the most popular summer resorts in the country, Ogunquit somehow maintains its early charm. Is it the old fishing shacks that still stand at Perkins Cove? Is it the Marginal Way, that famous walk open to the public along the tops of cliffs? Is it the beach, so long and wide that hundreds of vacationers can stretch out on its sands in uncrowded comfort?

Or is it the charm of its people who, when the summer visitors have gone, return to the quiet lives of their ancestors?

South Berwick

August 23, 1967

IF YOU WANT a few hours of respite from the coast's noises of traffic, the swish and crash of ocean, screams of joyous children, silver forever changing hands, golf clubs forever hitting golf balls – take a ride inland to tranquil South Berwick.

In olden times South Berwick was a thriving river port, with shipbuilding and lumber yards; two areas of town are still known as "The Landing." Came the time, just before the Civil War, when the building of wooden ships began its decline, and lumber was no longer in great demand. Then woolen and cotton started coming into the town with their mills, and shoes with their factories.

Now, except for one shoe factory, they have all left, lured by cheap labor and tax concessions of the South. The bulk of South Berwick's working citizens commutes to the Portsmouth Naval Yard or the General Electric Company at Somersworth, New Hampshire.

Still left in all their glory, however, and testifying to sturdy materials and the care used in their construction, are South Berwick's beautiful old homes. One of the loveliest is the Sarah Orne Jewett Mansion, built in 1774 and bought later by Sarah's grandfather, Captain Theodore Jewett. Sarah spent most of her life here, writing children's stories and books about Maine (*The Country of the Pointed Fir* is one) with the tenderness that has made them loved throughout the world.

Sarah never married and when she died a relative removed the contents of her house. Only her bedroom remained as it was when she lived. Her glasses still hang over her bed, her quill pen rests in its ink stand. In the closet are her umbrella and what is thought to be one of her gowns. She might have just stepped out of the room. "Sarah never really grew up," says a South Berwick woman familiar with the author's life. "She kept her toys till the day she died." The bedroom – with its dolls, school slate and other things dear to childhood – does indeed show a tendency to cling to a happy childish past.

The South Berwick Historical Society has assembled furniture of early periods for the rest of the house. The spacious central hall, extending from front to back, is among the loveliest in old homes of New England. Its woodwork, which took three shipbuilders a hundred days to carve, reveals the craftsmanship that so many of the early carpenters learned in their apprenticeship and never lost.

Another beautiful old building is the Chadbourne House, an outstanding example of Colonial architecture with carved woodwork and paneling and Indian shutters that slide out from the walls to cover the windows. When the Chadbourne House was built in 1670 it was said that there was no house north of it until Canada.

South Berwick, originally a part of Kittery, was separated from it in 1713 and remained one community till 1814 when it was divided into its present compass-point names.

Berwick Academy for boys is the oldest private school in Maine. It was founded in 1791 when Maine, as part of Massachusetts, could not even claim the statehood later achieved in 1820.

Here too is a private girls' academy, St. Joseph's, whose present administration building was once an ancient tavern. Lafayette is supposed to have visited it, although there is no more real proof of Lafayette's conviviality than of George Washington's going to sleep in all those houses.

Eliot

August 30, 1967

ELIOT'S HISTORY is tied up with that of Kittery. It was once a part of it. Now Eliot has its own government, its own schools – in other words its own identity.

It also has some of the loveliest backwoods country known to York County. Its roads wind through meadows and grasslands, farms and pastures, past houses of rare old vintage. You enter the Magic Mountain when you enter Eliot, or "Brigadoon," where a world of the past is opened up to the visitor on one magical day and night. You are out of all the pollutions — air, sound and neon — out of all the go-go tempo of your life. You are back in a time when life was leisurely, when it had slow rhythms, where old values were never questioned, and where people lived and died in firmly structured fashion.

It was the traders, coming to New England shores in 1624, who settled Eliot. Feelers were put out by major European countries in those early days. The French sent, surprisingly, an Italian navigator, one John Verrazani, and around the date 1600 English explorers came, including Captain John Smith. The new land held allure in spite of — perhaps because of — its dangers. It was a time of adventure in the world's history, when the men, whose counterparts today volunteer for space travel, unfurled their sails and pointed their frail barks toward the new land.

The first recorded settlement of the area was in 1623, started by Alexander Shapleigh and known as the Second Parish of Kittery down to the time when Eliot petitioned the Massachusetts General Court for incorporation into a township. The incorporation was approved in March of 1810.

Until 1850 the town grew slowly. It was, simply, a lovely rural town. It had no industry except the brick-making that seemed to flourish throughout early New England. But in 1919 "Green Acre" came into being and ever since Eliot has taken its place among the summer resorts of coastal Maine.

"Green Acre" originally was the home of Sarah Farmer, daughter of inventor Moses Farmer. She traveled widely and in her wanderings collected artistic people whom she brought back to her home, eventually making of it a literary center. Her "collection" comprised people of all faiths and out of them came the followers of Bahai, a sect which flourishes there today.

Eliot has the proper share of historic spots. In a small, green shingled cottage that nests in borders of old-fashioned flowers lives Juliette Worster, a direct descendant of Noah Emery who was First King's Council for the Province of Maine. He was born December 11th, 1699, and died almost to the day sixty-two years later, in 1761. His home, built probably by his father, was burned but the shingled cottage, which was his law office, still stands. Inside are his desk and a few chairs belonging to him, and some dishes that might have been his.

In Eliot too is "Ambush Rock," where on Sunday, July 4, 1697 (the date was yet to become a national holiday), Major Charles Frost, Phebe Littlefield Heard, wife of Captain John Heard, and Dennis Downing met their deaths. They had been attending divine service in Unity, in the precinct of Berwick, and were returning home on horseback when Indians jumped from behind the rock and attacked them.

And on the grounds of Lanier Inn, on one of Eliot's byways where the trees seem greener than green and the air especially fresh, is a marker that denotes the spot where William Everett's Tavern stood. It was here, on November 16, 1652, that the submission of Maine to Massachusetts was signed. Maine was not to be a state until 1820.

Go to Eliot some day. If you want to see a setting as nearly unspoiled as can be, a place where our country's forefathers lived and struggled and died, where trees canopy quiet lanes and flowers seem to grow taller and brighter than anywhere else, where serenity reigns—go. There are few such places left today.

Wells

July 15, 1968

QUIET, WOODSY Harriseeket Road in Wells was once the center of a bustling community back in the 1700s. It was also where the Maine sloop *Prosperous* brought a small group of Acadians when they were expelled from their land in Canada. (Have you read Longfellow's "Evangeline" lately?)

Wells was probably named for the cathedral town in England. It was a primitive community, as were most of them in the very early days. People worked harder than we today can ever realize. There was no time for the refinements, and there were no schools. Most of the inhabitants could not write their names. Houses were of logs and sparsely furnished. Edmund Littlefield, the richest man in town, did not own a single book. Joseph Cross owned a looking glass and a carpet but no chairs. Life was grim, and people found release where they could — often in rum and licentiousness. A fasting period was ordered by the church "because of sins, blastings, mildew, drought, grasshoppers, caterpillars, smallpox, and the low state of religion in all parts."

Add to this the constant threat of Indian attacks, sometimes caused, it must be admitted, by a tendency to cheat the red man of his lands. On Route One in Wells is a stone slab marking the site of the Storer Garrison House. It was erected "to commemorate the defense . . . by Capt. James Converse, twenty-nine Massachusetts soldiers, the neighborly yeomanry of Wells and various heroic women . . . [in] 1692, whereby 400 French and Indians were successfully resisted and Wells remained the Easternmost town in the provinces not destroyed by the enemy."

You are speeding past history in Wells. Slow down and stop for awhile!

Saco

September 1, 1971

THE SACO OF TODAY knows a peace it seldom had in its early days. The gracious homes lining its elm-shaded streets give little hint of the Indian attacks and wars that plagued the settlers, a price the white man had to pay for taking Indian land.

Picture what the banks of the Saco River looked like a mere 300 years ago. The forests are deep. The sun filters through pine and hemlock onto soft-pine-needle carpets. The rushing river tumbles past wigwams.

Sakokis, the young wife of Chief Squando, paddles across the river in her canoe. In the bottom of the craft sits her baby. A longboat of English sailors draws near. They overturn the canoe. The young mother flounders in Saco waters, struggling to save her child. (White men of the time believed Indians did not have to learn to swim, that they swam instinctively, like animals. It was to test this belief that the sailors upset the canoe.)

Sakokis rescued her baby but it died of exposure and Chief Squando vowed death to every white man within range of his tomahawk. Sakokis's revenge was quieter. She put a curse on the river. "As long as white men live by Saco waters three of their race must drown in them each year."

Whittier has captured her grief in a poem:

Squando shuts his eyes and sees,
Far off, Saco's hemlock trees,
In his wigwam, still as stone,
Sits a woman all alone,
Wampam beads and birchen strands
Dropping from her careless hands
Listening ever for the fleet
Patter of a dead child's feet.

It was sassafras that founded Saco and Biddeford and the Pool. Sassafrass, that fragrant medicinal root that sent a little ship hardly bigger than a lobster boat tossing over the Atlantic from England to take back a load of it for the cure of whatever gouty ills beset Britishers of the time.

When Captain Pring made this trip in the early 1600s, there was not a single white man's habitation on the whole eastern seaboard. He sailed his little craft up the Saco River for five miles—watched from behind trees no doubt by astonished Indians—plucked his cargo, and sailed down the river again to the open sea where he bobbed back over the ocean to home.

Such glowing accounts did he give on arrival home of the beauty of the area, it could be said he started the trend of tourism that has gone on ever since.

Up till 1718 there was just one big place called Saco. Then one side of the river became Biddeford (By-the-Ford) named for Bideford in England, the other side remaining Saco. In 1762 Saco's name was changed to Pepperellborough. It's easy to see—with the scarcity of parchment and people writing with scratchy quills and all—why Pepperellborough was changed back to Saco in 1805.

Biddeford is York County's major shopping center and Saco has some of the loveliest old Colonial homes hereabouts. Do your shopping in Biddeford and eat there some time this week, then make a leisurely tour of elm-shaded Main Street in Saco. Finish your day's adventure with a short but scenic ride to lovely Biddeford Pool where the Saco River meets the broad Atlantic.

Kennebunkport

June 14, 1972

IT'S HARD TO imagine, strolling among the gift shops and restaurants of Kennebunkport, that not so long ago there were no restaurants, just taverns. The town's only shops may have been a ship chandlery or two, perhaps a blacksmith's later on.

Shells of ships that were formed in shipyards up the Kennebunk River were floated down to the Port, fitted out and rigged there before they sailed off on lucrative trips to the Orient or to hunt the elusive whale.

Sea captains' and sailors' wives swept the dirt road with their long skirts and paced the widows' walks you can still see on some of the old Port houses, watching for a glimpse of white sail or glint of sun-caught brass on the horizon that meant a loved one, away from home perhaps two years, would soon be sailing into harbor.

A sturdy Kennebunk ship bore Audubon on his first voyage to England and another, the *Windemere*, carried as cabin boy H. M. Stanley, he who later was to explore Africa and find the lost Dr. Livingston.

Between 1800 and 1812, 22,000 tons of shipping were launched from the Port. The Kennebunks were known throughout the world as builders of the fleetest sailing ships ever to careen before a spanking breeze on the seven seas.

Now it is over. Although fine working and pleasure craft still are constructed in two private boat yards along the river, no longer do those large "proud ones" sway out to sea from the Port. No longer do sailors from home and foreign ports crowd the streets. But in winter sometimes in the silence, if your ear is attuned to such, you may hear the clank of an anchor chain echoing down through the years, the slapping of ratlines in a brisk breeze, or the faint "Hallo-o-o" of a seaman clinging high on a mast in those long-gone days, as he catches his first sight of home.

North Berwick

Undated

EARLY SETTLERS drifting into what is now York County knew nothing of urban planning, and had they known would have cared less. Survival was uppermost in their minds. They huddled together for safety against attack. It was more practical too, than a scattering of homes, for neighbors helped build your cabin, helped with the crops, and were near in time of distress.

Another survival technique was to settle beside a stream. Water made you relatively secure from attack on one side at least, water and fish were readily available (especially needed if the community was under siege), and in the absence of roads water transport was at your door.

Then came small industries that settled by the river because it furnished power, and settled in the town because they were thus within walking distance for their employees. This is why the center of so many Maine towns has a factory, a "skyscraper" which is often reflected in the river at its feet. The river, incidentally, in most cases also bisects the town.

North Berwick is such a town. The banks of its Great Works River bear a small factory, not a noisy one; the town is hardly wakened by it when it starts operations in the morning.

In fact, because of the patina of quiet and antiquity overlying North Berwick, it is hard to think of the town as a busy one with thriving industries. But a successful line of shoes is manufactured here. Here too is a wire and cable industry with far-flung markets. And here is where bleachers are made that go to stadiums and gymnasiums throughout the world.

Part of the town's aura of tranquility is achieved by slow-paced inhabitants who will not let themselves be infected by the "City tempo" of their coastwise neighbors. Part is due to its ancient oaks and elms. And part to many of its gracious homes that have been standing since the 18th and 19th centuries.

Old homes on the York County coast are pretty well documented by now, and cleaned out from attic to underpinnings. But in the hinterland, on rivers where early settlers built their homes, there still may be found evidences of Maine's storied past.

2

People

Silvio Bernier in his wheelchair in front of the Lafayette Elm /
After a 1962 photo by the author

Sylvio Bernier

August 16, 1962

ON MAY 29, 1957, a new patient arrived at the Leech Nursing Home on Storer Street in Kennebunk. The ambulance door opened and a medium-sized, brown-eyed man, handled like a fragile doll, was moved into the house and placed in a bed. The man reportedly had only six months to live. He was almost stone deaf. He was suffering extreme pain. When the sheet touched his swollen body he screamed.

So Sylvio Bernier, fifty-five years old, started on nursing home routine: thermometer under the tongue, torturous bathing of the edematous body, visit from the doctor, medication, motionless through the long day, and another dawn to wait for in another night when drugs could only touch the edge of pain.

But this was not for Sylvio. He had been strong and well. He would do his best to make himself strong again. As a youth he had trained with dumbbells until he could lift fifty-pound weights, then seventy-five, then a hundred to three-hundred pounds.

Remembering this, Sylvio started flexing his crippled fingers. The pain was more than he could bear. He rested. He flexed again, and rested. A little more each time, a little more each day. Next came the limbs. He stretched, panting with agony, and stretched again.

A year from the day Sylvio entered the nursing home he was in a wheel chair. And that was the beginning of a second life for Sylvio Bernier.

Have you driven or walked along Storer Street lately? Storer Street, boasting the famous Lafayette Elm, is the cleanest street in town. You'll see a bright-eyed man plying a broom up and down the sidewalks. All spring, all summer, and all fall he works, sweeping dust and dirt and fallen leaves into neat piles and gathering them into a basket.

Is it hard work?

"It was at first," says Sylvio. "Still is. But I'm happiest when I work. The more I work the better I feel."

He does everything for himself. The time the nurses used to spend bathing the tortured body can now be used on other patients because Sylvio bathes himself. Socks and clothes that once took half an hour to draw on over the sensitive skin are now managed by Sylvio. His knife and fork he lifts slowly with still-crippled fingers, but he won't let anyone else do it for him.

If you don't see him sweeping the street, you may see him in his wheel chair in front of the nursing home, smoking his pipe and waving or talking to a growing army of friends, or carving copies of the Liberty Bell or the figure of a favorite nurse. To exercise his stiffened fingers, Sylvio has taken up mechanical drawing and carving. This is a talent he didn't know he had; it emerged from his determination to be strong again.

And if you don't see him sweeping or carving, he is probably "taking a walk." This means wheeling his chair around town by himself, looking in the shop windows, greeting friends, and keeping up with the town gossip. Last week he wheeled himself up past the high school and back, a distance of nearly a mile.

How does he manage? How does he cross the street?

"Oh, I know all the cops. If they're not on hand, someone will do it."

And the winters—are they a time of idleness?

Far from it. "There's always something to do inside," says Sylvio. "Work in the laundry or sweeping the floors. I always find things to do."

For recreation Sylvio plays cards and checkers. He's a crack checker player and takes on all comers. If anyone reading this would care to be trounced, Sylvio invites him to come and pass an hour at the game, Or, if you prefer, you can lose at Five Hundred, cribbage, poker, Canfield, even tiddlywinks. Name it and you can go down, beaten by a man who is a winner.

A winner, too, at life.

The picture of Sylvio (here sketched from original photograph in the *Star*) shows him in his wheelchair in front of Kennebunk's logo, The Lafayette Elm. Both are gone now, each the victim of a disease, each having lived longer than is expected of humans or trees that have been beset by fatal illness. Had the onset of Sylvio's sickness started today, when curative miracles abound, he might still be alive.

As it was, his own courage and determination extended his life. The Lafayette Elm succumbed to Dutch elm disease. Only a tree, but it too fought. Man, tree, and every living organism have within them the natural elements for survival, to be nourished or not, as the victim decides.

Nubble Light

August 18, 1965

YOU CAN DRAW a line from Bald Head Cliff to Brave Boat Harbor on the southern Maine coast and it will be almost straight except for a spit of land that projects like a finger for a mile out into the Atlantic. The nail of the finger is Nubble Light (at Cape Neddick), a beacon maintained by the Coast Guard, one of the few remaining lighthouses still not automated. At high tide the Nubble is separated from the mainland by deep and turbulent waters. At low tide you can walk across, although the walk is a little on the scrambly side.

It was at the turn of the tide when we climbed down the boulders forming the end of Cape Neddick peninsula and waded across to the island through water so clear every barnacle shone white as a popcorn. Halfway across we met people coming back. "No visitors," they said, passing. "They don't want us over there." Not having a press badge we held high our note book to indicate our errand and waded on.

We beached, scrambled up a pebbly incline to an empty boathouse and turned right onto a flight of steps, passing under a NO VISITORS sign that hung over the first step. Was a reporter a visitor? We mounted anyway. We wish now we had counted those steps. We went up and down them six times that afternoon.

At the top, we were high above the sea. The rock formation we stood on was covered with grass. On one side of us, cliffs plunged to wet black rocks far below. On the other side was the mainland. We paused for a moment to get our breath and watched the movements of the fishing men (as opposed to fishermen) over there, the picnickers, the just plain sitters. Does everyone on islands get this feeling of having removed himself from the mainstream of life? And that the mainstream is unimportant and the rushing-about of people in it resembles compulsive movements of ants?

A dangerous state of mind. We walked toward the house. Another short flight of steps and we were knocking at the door. The corner of our eye saw a blue glow and we heard a TV. A pretty Oriental girl of about eighteen appeared in the doorway. "*You're* the lighthouse keeper?" we asked.

She dimpled. "No. That's my stepfather. He's in Portsmouth. Will you come in?"

Inside, a Western was going full blast. Beside the chair, where the girl had been curled up watching it—her imprint sill hollowed the cushion—was a basket. In it, a tiny Oriental baby waved fists at us, influenced no doubt by the Western.

The girl, Billy Emmont, is part Japanese. She and her baby, four months old, are visiting mother Jeanne Matsuo and stepfather Wilson Eugene (Gene) Allen and their son, her stepbrother, Wilson Eugene Allen II. While the family was shopping in Portsmouth, Billy was keeping the light; the day being clear, this was no chore at all. The folks would be back sometime during the afternoon because Gene had to turn the light on fifteen minutes before sunset. In the meantime, Billy would show us around.

In the basement, a whitewashed 5,000-gallon tank held rainwater for the family's use. If the tank runs dry—it could in weather such as we've been having—the Coast Guard Cutter *Cowslip* brings more.

The electric switch in the basement that turns on and off the rotating beacon looked like any household switch. Its cabinet impressed us more, painted vivid blue with a Chinese red door against the white wall. We were admiring it when something suddenly occurred to us.

"The tide comes in pretty fast here, doesn't it?" we asked Billy. She shrugged. She hadn't been here long enough to know much about the tides.

A picture niggled at our mind. Gene, Jeanne, and Junior walk along the streets of Portsmouth, their marketing done. A movie marquee catches their eye. The three of them huddle. "Billy can turn the Light on this once," Gene says. They go in. Meanwhile, back at the lighthouse, caught by the tide, we sit far into the night watching TV.

This part of the picture frightened us. We ran out of the house, down the steps, and waded across to the mainland. The tide now crawled toward our knees. Scramble up the boulders and to the car. No keys. They are in our bag, back there on the couch at the lighthouse.

Scramble down the boulders again, wade across, run the steps, into the house, grab the bag. "We'll wait on the mainland for your family," we shout over our shoulder at Billy. This time across, the tide lapped at our knees. Back on the mainland, we sank on the rocks to dry off and wait for the Allens' return.

In a short time their pink and grey Ford drew up. Jeanne Allen put her purchases into a box which Billy pulled across to the island on overhead wires. We had had to get permission to visit the light from the Coast Guard group commander in South Portland, so the Allens had been expecting us, and once again we crossed the inlet, this time in a boat.

At the house we enjoyed the Coke and cookies Jeanne brought us with true Oriental hospitality (she is of Japanese extraction), then set out on a tour of the island with Gene, Jeanne, and Gene Junior (who answers when these three call to one another?). Junior, an enchanting jet-eyed, black-haired two-year-old, has a vocabulary consisting mainly of the last two words you have just uttered.

We walked the covered corridor to the beacon. "How long have you been on the light?" we asked Gene Senior.

("The wight," said Junior.)

"Since January 28th." Gene hails from West Virginia and talks with a slight drawl. "We came here from Mt. Desert Rock at Southwest Harbor. That's the farthest light out in the Atlantic. Twenty-two miles at sea. We were there for two years. I'm glad to be off it. Part of the rock—the part that had the generator house on it—got washed away in the hurricane of sixty-two."

("Cane sixee two"— Junior.)

Have you always been in the Coast Guard?"

("Toast hard.")

"No, just since February of fifty-seven. I was in the Marine Corps before I joined the Coast Guard. My old division is in Vietnam right now. Third Marine Division."

"Do you wish you were with them?"

"No, I'm glad to be right where I am."

Right where he was at the moment was in the light tower, located on the north part of the island rock, latitude 43 09.9, longitude 70 35.5. Below us the Atlantic spread its blue sparkle around the island and threw spume lace on the rocks like a fussy dressmaker, rearranged it, drew it off, tried it again. Straight down, the small shelter that houses the emergency generator looked like a red wooden block that might have been thrown onto the green sward by Junior. Beside us slept the huge glass eye. In a few hours it would wake up, blink, and sweep its beam the long night through.

Gene turns the light on fifteen minutes before sunset, turns it off fifteen minutes after sunrise. How does he know the exact moment the sun will rise and set? The Maine Sea Coast Mission furnishes him with a tide-sunset-sunrise table. All he has to do is add or subtract fifteen.

A group flash of the beacon occurs red every fifteen seconds, like this:

5 second light
2 second eclipse
2 second light
2 second eclipse
2 second light
2 second eclipse

The bell for fog is struck every fifteen seconds. The bell is a new one, incidentally. The old one was moved out about three years ago and now rests in the park opposite the Ocean House at Long Sands.

The beacon is 88 feet above the water, its candlepower 6000. It is visible for 15 miles. The top of the lantern is 41 feet from the ground. The light was built in 1879. Its lens was made in Paris in 1891 (presumably, before that, the lamp was lit by oil).

We glanced again at the "ants" on the mainland. Picnicking ants, fishing ants, some just sitting ants. A lot of them had cameras, aimed at the Lighthouse. "Why aren't visitors allowed on the island anymore?" we asked Gene.

"Vandalism. That and stealing from the boathouse at low tide, so the group commander ordered no more visitors. Maybe they'll let them come again some day. I don't know."

We started to climb down the stairs. "What do you do all winter?"

("All winter"— Junior.)

There is plenty to do, it seems. Just painting the lighthouse and dwellings and keeping them in apple-pie order take a lot of time. Jeanne helps her husband in this. The first time she went out on the catwalk to paint she was frightened. And the paint kept blowing back in her face and hair. Now she's more used to it. (Later she showed us a hand cream that removes paint but does not dry the skin.)

We were at ground level now and we looked up. Lighthouse stairways, we think, are among the world's prettiest— light, delicate, spiralling skyward as if magnetized by that life-saving gem at the top.

On our way back through the corridor we noticed a government sign: GOOD HOUSEKEEPING IS THE KEYNOTE TO SAFETY. CLEANLINESS, ORDER, AND A PLACE

FOR EVERYTHING ARE ESSENTIALS OF SAFETY, a sign that could hang to advantage in many a home.

In February, last winter, the Allens were marooned on their island for five days during a storm. Once when a wave broke over the house, Gene tried to take Jeanne and Gene Junior to the tower but Jeanne refused to go. "It was only once," she told us, "only one wave."

How did they feel, trapped, while the storm screamed around them? "It wasn't so bad," Gene said. "One of the previous keepers was marooned here for ten days."

If shore power goes off for any reason, the emergency generator automatically takes over. It is kept warm for immediate starting. (We put our hand on it; it was warm.)

It was time to leave. Any more questions would have to wait. We wanted to ask what kept Jeanne's shining black hair from turning white when Junior races like a lemming to the edge of the cliffs, as he tried to do several times while we were there. The Allens' German Shepherd limped from a fall he'd had off the cliff just the day before, his second fall. The Allens felt it was miraculous he hadn't been killed.

We wanted to know too how it feels in winter to be in a lighthouse with the wind howling outside, to know the mainland to be only a stone's throw away, but a million miles if it had to be reached by dory in a storm.

We tucked these questions into our mind's tuck-away compartment. We descended the pebbly incline while Jeanne cranked the boat down the ways. We climbed into it and Gene started to row. The German Shepherd swam before us. He always does this. It is one of his duties, he feels, to part the waters for the boat. Everybody works at a lighthouse.

We looked back. Jeanne and Junior and Billy, the baby in her arms, were waving goodbye. The white tower and the white dwelling picked up pink tints from the lowering sun. The generator house glowed like a garnet. We turned and faced the shore.

We were about to rejoin the ants.

Lighthouses along the Maine coast, now almost entirely automated, are catalogued according to their usefulness to marine traffic. The lighthouses of Boon and Isles of Shoals, for example, are rated Category 1 because of their remote distance from land, which in this case would be the Maine and New Hampshire coastal boundary.

Nubble light is in Category 2, meaning that at this date she is *partially* automated. Her light is always on and the rolling in of fog—that terror of ancient and present-day mariners — sets off her foghorn. And what if the light malfunctions? "You have to rely on someone going by who'll notice it," says Tim Bass who as a member of the South Portland Coast Guard continually inspects the nine southern Maine lighthouses in his domain. "They'll phone some town official," Bass goes on, "and he'll call us and we'll take care of the problem." (But not so fast, it can be assumed, as would a live-in keeper.)

Category 3 lighthouses are fast diminishing as automation proceeds — or as they are being turned over to the towns in which they operated — or as they are saved as relics of the past by local conservation or historic groups.

Also in Category 3 is Goat Island lighthouse off Kennebunkport. This small island's only structures are the lighthouse and its adjoining keeper's house, now vacated. Because of its part in President Bush's security network the light, operated chiefly for commercial fishermen, is activated now by radar ashore. Automation was expected in the summer of 1991.

For those purists who decry the passing of the man-operated lighthouse — take comfort. There remains a non-automated and functional memento in the form of Boston Harbor lighthouse and its live keeper. This is owing to the efforts of Massachusett's Senator Ted Kennedy to maintain the light's historic integrity.

Mildred Day

September 15, 1965

WE HADN'T MET her yet, but we thought the interview with so old a lady as Mildred Day would go better at our home than in the turbulent offices of the *Star*, so we made the arrangements with her niece, Mrs. Jacobs of Biddeford, also a stranger to us, who picked her up and brought her to us. Two women got out of the car, and we peered behind them to see where the old lady might be.

Mildred Day, at seventy-nine, is tall and walks upright. She wore a pink sweater slung casually over a light blue dress, white beads around her neck and white button earrings. She laughs a lot. We learned later in the interview that she reads and sews without glasses. So much for the "old" part of "old lady."

What is the secret of this agelessness? Perhaps teaching forty-nine years in the same one-room schoolhouse and perhaps keeping nine grades quiet in that one room. Perhaps the three miles to and from school that she walked. Or perhaps the work of keeping the schoolhouse itself going: "I was janitor too. Our only heat came from a wood-burning stove and I had to keep it stoked. I shoveled snow until snow ploughs came into use. That relieved me of a lot of physical labor."

All those forty-nine years (except one, in Lyman) were spent in the Durrell School in Arundel, now a firehouse. She herself had attended Durrell from age five until she went to Kennebunk High School. After completing high school in 1903, she specialized in English in Rochester Business College, took summer courses at Gorham Normal and studied music for two years. When she became a teacher she put all her learning to work, including her music. A secondhand piano she bought injected a little fun into the pupils' daily study grind when she played and they sang.

Her hardest problem? Keeping eight other grades busy and quiet while she taught one. We thought this would be downright impossible, but Mildred Day had a voice of authority, according to her niece. She also had a ruler which on rare occasions came down on the knuckles of misbehavers. Usually, though, a good tongue-lashing did the trick. "Not even whispering was allowed," said Mildred Day.

Did she ever use the ruler on Lincoln Spencer (recently appointed State Superior Court Judge)? A scandalized look crossed her face. "Heavens no! Why, I would no more have thought of disciplining Lincoln when he was a child than I'd think of it this minute," she said. "None of the four Spencer children ever needed punishing."

We wanted to know why so many grades were crowded into one room. "I guess schools weren't considered so important in the early days. At least the conditions children studied under weren't given the attention they are now." Once the town closed one of its schools and sent her forty more pupils to be jammed in with the others like sardines. The closed school was reopened shortly after the school board paid a visit to Mildred Day's classroom and watched her walking sideways up and down the aisles, inching her way through a small sea of pupils. Mrs.Jacobs, herself a teacher, spoke up to say that the average number of pupils in today's classroom is twenty-five to thirty; grades are rarely combined.

Crowded, chaotic but for a firm hand, demanding great stamina and energy on the part of the teacher, the old one-room schoolhouse still held satisfactions. "At least," said Mildred Day, "I was monarch of all I surveyed." She tried to inspire her pupils and she has followed them through life with intense interest. She still hears from many of them and now that she's retired not a few come to visit her.

"What have I done since retirement? Oh, dear, that's a hard one. I never did develop a hobby. I guess entertaining all my grandnieces and nephews and a few great-grand ones is my hobby."

She has always lived on a farm; not a working farm now, but she and her sister and brother-in-law (the Harry Gowens) and another brother-in-law (Mr. Grant) still keep Jersey cows. Miss Day has two thoroughbred horses, and "I'd hate to have to count the kittens." She thought a moment. "I guess you could say my hobbies are children, horses, dogs and cats—in that order."

Nine of the nineteen who graduated with her from K.H.S. in 1903 still live in the Kennebunk area. Once a year they meet for a reunion and one of their number, George Fiske, takes them out in his boat. Mildred Day takes "seasick pills."

After her death the elementary school where Mildred had taught in Arundel (adjacent to Kennebunk) was renamed for her. It is now the Mildred L. Day Memorial School.

Mountain Preacher

December 4, 1968

HE IS CALLED the "Mountain Preacher" because he has spent most of his preaching life on Mt. Agamenticus in York. He is a simple man, honest and direct and full of love for God and his fellow man. It appears sometimes that the Lord sends tragedy to those who love Him best (because they seem more able to take it?).

Reverend C. Stanley Stevens left his home on the mountain at 7:15 A.M. last Sunday to walk the few yards to his church, the Friendly Christian Tabernacle. He was going to start a fire in the stove for worshippers who would arrive later for the service.

Halfway there he heard his wife shout into the still mountain air, "Stan! It's on fire!" Turning, he saw smoke and flames licking out from around windows and doors of his house – it was that sudden. Noise at the back meant that their sons, the two of their eight grown children who still live at home, were clambering down the ladder from the attic where they had been sleeping. Kicking open the back door they ran out clad only in their trousers; then, fighting smoke, they made their way back again, one to sound the alarm, the other to grab boxes containing their parents' wedding license and the deeds to the house and the Tabernacle. That was all they could manage. By the time the York Beach, York Village, and Ogunquit fire departments could wind up the mountain road there was no stopping the flames until they had run their course at about 9:15.

Stanley Stevens's wife Eunice began to cry. The last straw was her piano, one of her most prized possessions, now a blackened ruin. Her glasses, melted and broken, still lay on top. "I put my arm around her," the Reverend told this reporter. "I couldn't have a better woman, much better than I deserve. She's beautiful – I don't mean Marilyn Monroe beautiful." He is rich, he says, only in his family, his love of his fellow man, and his faith. He has never had money. He supplements his pay for preaching, which comes from the offerings of his small congregation, by working at gardening for other people, raking leaves, and the like. Not easy, one would think, for a man crippled at thirty-seven by polio (he is now in his middle fifties). But even this disease he considers a blessing because it enabled him to know how the sick feel. "My most important work now," he says, "is praying at bedsides in the hospitals. I don't care what denomination the sick are. A hospital is no place to talk religion. I was sick for a year once myself. I know what it's like."

The son of an Episcopalian mother and a Congregationalist father, he became converted to his interdenominational Christian faith when he was sixteen. "My education has been limited. I'm ordained, though. I founded the Tabernacle out of necessity because I wanted a place to worship in. And I love the people here on the mountain. I never lost the calling. It was years ago and I had a wife and a nine-month-old baby, and I'd been getting only two dollars and fifty cents a week preaching. I didn't know what to do so I prayed and it seemed to me a voice told me to go to the Bible. It opened by chance at Micah 6:1. 'Contend thou before the mountains, and let the hills hear thy voice.' So I preached at Agamenticus Church and on Sunday afternoons and Thursday nights at the Beech Ridge Free Will Baptist Church—that's near Beaver Dam Grange Hall. And then I built the Tabernacle."

With the onset of polio Mr. Stevens became a quadruple paralytic. He still cannot raise his left arm, and his right one was rigid for nearly seven years. When he falls, he can get up only with help. If he were young, he says he'd build another house on the ashes of the old. He is no stranger to carpentry. He constructed, among other things, his house, the Tabernacle, the parsonage of the Agamenticus Church, and even, when workmen could not be found to do it, its steeple.

The family will live temporarily in the parsonage of the Agamenticus Church. A "Stevens Fund" has been started at the First National Bank of Portland branches in York and Ogunquit. Food and clothing are being collected through York's Community Service Organization.

"I don't know how to thank everybody," says Stanley Stevens, "for all they are doing."

He preached a service the night after the fire took his home. "Not many showed up," he said. "They probably thought there wouldn't be any service." We told him of people who talk of him as a truly Christ-like man who lives only to help others. "Please," he begged, "don't make me out anything special. I want my Savior to have any credit due. I have got a wonderful God." He quoted the Bible again: "All things work together for good to those who love God and are called according to his purpose."

It was very cold on the mountain. Reverend Stevens's hands were shaking. He climbed into the car of a friend who had driven into the yard, and we walked over to the Tabernacle. Its inside was bare of pews: straight-backed wooden chairs are used. A stove stood toward the back of the room. Stacked under windows at one side was a cord or more of wood. Bright hand-painted posters with religious themes hung on the walls. A few chairs bore donations of blankets, clothes, etc., for the Stevenses. On the floor about a dozen packing boxes held clothing, brought annually to the church for Eunice Stevens to send to the poor elsewhere. In spite of the family's own need right now, the boxes are still to be sent away.

Two of the sons were in the church. "What do you think your father will do now?" we asked.

One said, "He'll make out OK."

"He's done it before," said the other.

The Reverend C. Stanley Stevens still lives on Mt. Agamenticus. After the fire he moved into the house he had built for his parents who had died. He preached in his Friendly Christian Tabernacle until illness made him stop, but he hopes to get back to preaching. The church still functions during summers as a meeting place for Alcoholics Anonymous every Tuesday night.

In spite of what he hopes is only a temporary retirement, the Reverend is far from inactive. CB (Citizen Band) radio keeps him busy sending religious messages of support "all over the country and sometimes Canada." Once he "just happened" to get through to Italy—it was having one of its earthquakes—for an Italian woman in Berwick who worried about her relative's safety. And once he talked for half an hour with a family in Kansas that he thought desperately needed religious help. What form does the help take? "I pray with them and end up singing a religious song."

He has been married fifty-nine years to Eunice, "a wonderful woman. She'd have to be wonderful to have gone through what she's had to."

Our telephone interview ended with his saying, "Don't make this sound too ritzy. I'm just an old country preacher." Then the "old country preacher" said a prayer for us and sang a song.

The Standishes' Waiting Room

June 4, 1969

"HOW DO YOU STAND IT?" "We hardly notice it. We sleep right through the night."

This dialogue took place in Kennebunk's abandoned railroad station with its new owners, John and Carol Standish, who have lived there since April with their small daughter Elana. The train, it seemed for an awful moment, had jumped its tracks, was heading straight for us. But it only shook the building and passed by, its roar diminishing as it sped north.

Are they afraid Elana in an unguarded moment might run onto the tracks? "No," said her mother, who is expecting another child in August. "She's been taught a little song, 'Only trains go on the tracks. I go on the street.'" She laughed. "Of course, streets really aren't much safer."

Elana, a three-year-old blond bomb, who could challenge any galloping train, was named for a full-blooded Indian the Standishes met in Canada and grew to love. "She was the most gentle, kind person we'd seen in a long time," Carol said. "Completely unspoiled. And this one," she nodded her head at Elana II who was tricycling around the floor at 150 mph, "turns out to be entirely the opposite."

John Standish attended Brown University, Carol went to Middlebury. Running a small craft shop in Cambridge, Massachusetts, decided them on having their own, preferably in Maine. Carol says, "Ever since we were married – that's four and a half years ago – we've been looking for land up here. I love this area and so does John. My parents had a place in Biddeford Pool. Now they're in York. So I'm familiar with it. When we heard about this, we came up to look at it last winter. It was just before Christmas. Mr. Brown (of the *Big E*) had a lot of antiques stored in it. The windows were broken, and it was cold and bleak."

But youth falls in love with what gives age pause. The Standishes bought the station and began work on it the first of the year. The baggage room was turned into a living room with a sleeping loft halfway up to the high ceiling. John, who has done all the carpentry, cut a hallway through the end of what was the Ladies Room, using the remainder as their own bathroom. The Men's Room became a bedroom for Elana. During the winter an old coal stove, which they cooked on, furnished their heat. The fire is out now for the summer; they cook on an electric plate in the kitchen, separated from the living room by room dividers.

The Waiting Room is their shop. Customers entering the "Kennebunk Railroad Station Craft Workshop" will see leaded stained-glass lamps, sconces, and window hangings; stoneware,pottery casseroles, vases and mugs; leather skirts, handbags, sandals, and silver jewelry. The leaded stained-glass objects are made by John who, incidentally, is descended from Plymouth colony's Captain Miles Standish—a genealogical fact we learned not from John but from a cooperative grapevine. The present-day Standish is a gentle, dark-haired young man with brown eyes and moustache, for whom stained glass holds a special enchantment. "And we don't even know if the craft has a name," says his wife. "It must have had in the past, when so much was done with it in medieval churches, but we don't know what to call it now." John doubts if there are even any courses in it. "The way to learn is to attach yourself to someone who knows."

In Cambridge, John met a San Franciscan whose interest in stained glass triggered his own. "There is so much to it," he says. "I make my design on paper. But if you're doing a ten thousand dollar church window, you draw on a big piece of glass with something like a magic marker. Then you start cutting colored glass and you set the pieces in with a kind of paraffin. You keep changing them around until you get the effect you want." John's own method makes use of a lightbox with a translucent plastic on top and a light underneath.

The Waiting Room shop is furnished with odds and ends made functional by the couple's ingenuity. An echo from the past is the ring of the same cash register that was used when trains still stopped at Kennebunk. "One of its buttons is labeled 'Pool,'" Carol said. "Did they have pool tables here? We'd love to find an old-timer who could answer all our questions."

A last nostalgic item: Newspapers are still dropped off at the station. They are brought by truck now, but the plop of the packages can still be heard. "Force of habit," suggests John. "Or maybe it's the protection of the overhanging eaves."

What was once the "Kennebunk Depot" in the distant past and now serves as outlet store and corporate offices for the renowned products of

"Tom's of Maine," was more than two decades ago the home of the Standishes as written above.

What has become of this family? They now number four, Jessica having joined the "blond bomb" Elana. They live in a house John himself built at Land's End at Cape Porpoise, "looking out on Vaughn's Island on one side and Paddy Creek on the other." The project took three years, but this did not keep the Standishes from living in it meanwhile. It boasts more room and certainly less noise than did the depot which, though not catering to travelers, still sees a once-a-day transport of goods.

John is finished with glass staining. He now thinks of it as a "wonderful retirement hobby" that will keep him busy during retirement. After giving it up, he worked in the construction business for eight years, has been assistant manager for Port Hardware for three. Carol has had her own framing business in Wharf Lane for eight years. John is not one to overflow with information about himself but we have learned that he authored *The Kennebunk Railroad Station Stained Glass Primer.* Meanwhile, the depot shop grew and became a success. Besides John's glasswork, room was made for Carol's pottery and craftwork of their friends, and John's windows decorate several edifices in the area. No doubt there will be more when he returns to his original love affair with stained glass.

Rocky Gorge Atelier

August 12, 1970

PROBABLY AS EARLY AS 1611, settlers from England started a sawmill just outside of what is now the Town of South Berwick. Indians, seeing the gang saws, said admiringly to the white men, words that translated into "Great works." The name has stuck.

The area is on a river that is also called Great Works. The river starts around Sanford, from Bauneg Beg Pond, and in ten miles or so reaches the sea at Portsmouth. At Great Works it tumbles two hundred feet over

The old Rocky Gorge woolen and processing mill in its early stages of restoration as the Rocky Gorge Atelier / After a 1970 photo by the author

two falls that are a short way apart. Before the falls were built the river was tidal a good distance, allowing ships from Portsmouth Harbor up almost as far as Great Works and making it in effect an inland seaport.

The sawmill had its day. Then, before the Civil War, a seven-building complex was erected for the manufacture of wool. The buildings, on both sides of the river, were joined across the water by a bridge, once part of a road to Portsmouth. (The road can still be seen.) Dating from about 1900 the buildings were called the "Rocky Gorge Woollen Mills," and up until fifteen years ago were functional. Somewhere along the line the name was changed to "Rocky Gorge Processing Company" when the mills were used for reclaiming old wool.

This company then went South seeking cheap labor. Taxes stopped, the town took over, and the buildings were rented to chicken farmers who did little or nothing to keep them in repair. In time they too left, and the huge complex was abandoned.

Boys began throwing rocks. No pane was left unshattered. Glass splinters glinted the excrement and sawdust left on the floors. Open to the elements, floor boards gave way; their ragged ends jutted out of widening holes. Weeds, occasionally a wild flower, grew out of the rotting wood. Equipment rusted. Outside, the river threaded its way to the sea through generations of cultch that had been tossed into it by mill occupants.

Into this rubble, one day late last winter, walked a young man. The destruction created by man and the elements registered on his eye and mind, but clearer was the vision of what the mill would be when he was done with it: an art school in the old atelier tradition, where novices would observe and learn from master painters and sculptors and craftsmen. A place where they could work and display their works, a place providing for communication among members of all the art disciplines. Himself an artist, the young man knew the value of quiet and space and the inspiration furnished by working in the company of others.

The mill had quiet. It had space. And the dream enabled him to look beyond the jagged panes to the lacy cascade of waterfall; to the trees, now hung with snow, that in summer etch their green tracery against the sky; to the beauty of the placid stream above the falls; to the rock cliffs the buildings rested on, cliffs that plunged sixty feet to the gorge. In his mind, Hayes had already renamed the mill "Rocky Gorge Atelier."

Ronald Hayes was born in Boston. He is an honors graduate from the Massachusetts College of Art (where he now teaches) and received his master's degree from the Boston School of the Museum of Fine Arts and Tufts University. He is thirty-five, has a wife and two children, Joshua, eight, Justina, one. He has been living summers for the past ten years in Kennebunkport but loves the South Berwick area so much he hopes by the end of next summer to be living there.

He had not come to view the mills alone last winter. With him were students from the Massachusetts College of Art to help clean up. "We started right away," he said. (It is now August and he is interrupting his work to take a *Star* reporter on a tour of the complex. He is stripped to the waist, shining with sweat. He looks happy.) "Through the winter we moved out literally tons of waste—sawdust, chicken excrement, rotted wood, glass, old machinery." The machinery caused him some pangs. Much was good, some of it made in the past century. "I contacted about every historical society around, woollen mills too, to see if they wanted it. Finally we had to break it up and take it away."

A few pieces of the machinery will stay. The gigantic horizontal turbine in the basement, for example, that powered the machinery when the mills were operational, will have a walk around it so visitors may see it in its original position and look beyond it to the base of the falls. The boiler equipment will stay too. Hayes moved it out of the office, adjacent to the main building, and into the mill. Each boiler weighed a thousand pounds. "I'll keep them to heat the building eventually. It would cost $10,000 to try to replace them today." He wants to set up a room in the atelier for artifacts and historical "leavings" of the buildings. Elizabeth Goodwin, caretaker of the Sarah Orne Jewett House, is researching the historic site and buildings, and Hayes would like anyone knowing anything about them to come forward with information.

All the buildings had been joined by pipes and wires. These are coming down by acetylene torch. "One day we came across two nests of starlings in the wires. We stopped work for two weeks to give them time to leave. The workmen thought I was crazy." Hayes stopped on the tour for a moment. He looked around at what still had to be taken care of—the rotted timbers, gaping holes in the floor, windows yet to be replaced—and quoted softly, "This time, Lord, you gave me a mountain . . . "

But he has experience converting old places and is undaunted. What troubles him at the moment is funds. His own money—from his earnings, from the sale of his patent on polymer paints, from a book he wrote, *The Art of Polymer Painting*—has financed the project up to a short time ago. He needs $30,000 to push construction so the school may be in operation by next summer. "Banks generally haven't wanted anything to do with it," he says cheerfully. "A couple of them looked but couldn't visualize what it would be."

So he has been doing it himself. He has replaced three hundred panes of glass and has "uncounted numbers to go." He has repainted the roofs, installed new dormers, fixed all the windows, is turning the mill office into living quarters. The mill is of wood outside reinforced with brick inside to carry the heavy equipment. Hayes is using all wooden construction. Once the building is sound, he says, he plans to approach various sources in an effort to come up with financial backing enough to finish the job.

The townspeople have shown interest. "They stop by to see what's going on." Boy Scouts have made a start on clearing the river of trash. Abutters to the property have contributed time and help. "Mr. Ottner of the Planning Board comes by and lifts my morale," says Hayes. "'You're doing a good job,' he'll say."

The tour ended. Hayes opened his "Blue Book," a loose-leaf notebook containing facts, figures, and photographs of work progress. On the first page were a few printed lines, cut from a book and pasted in: "Whatever you can do, or dream you can, begin it. Boldness has genius, power and magic in it." It is a quotation from Goethe. It is what brings Hayes's dream back into focus when life sometimes blurs it.

No further information is available.

Sylvie Dagher

August 25, 1971

MEET SYLVIE DAGHER, twenty-two, of Lebanon, visiting the Kennebunks under Rotary auspices. This is her first trip to the United States, thus her first to Maine, and she is getting the full treatment from her host families—picnics, sight-seeing, beaching, Rotary lunches, shopping in Portland, boating on the ocean ("I spent the night on the Downing boat") and she even turned lobster (wo)man when Howard Noyes took her out in his boat while he pulled in his traps.

Was she seasick? No. "There is the smell," she said in her lilting Middle-East accent, "but when you are on the sea you are not disturbed by it . . . " She had fun, she said, guessing how many lobsters would come up in each trap and watching the procedure of measuring. And then it was only a short step from "producer" to consumer—she ate her first lobster soon afterward. Lebanon, like most parts of the world, has crayfish, sometimes called crawfish, but it seems no other area than our Northeast has the unique breed of lobster we know.

Sylvie's trip to the United States is a dream come true; she has wanted to come for a long time. Not only is the visit turning out to be instructional, but she says she is having a marvelous time in Maine. At home she is too busy for much fun. She is a lawyer, with a BA in law and political science and an MA in law. She is readying herself for a thesis which, since her field of interest is public law, she thinks will be written on international maritime law.

As for outside interests—mainly music. She plays the piano, "classical only." But she and her brother both enjoy hearing all kinds, pop too. Her brother, twenty, is a chess and bridge enthusiast and plans to be an electronics engineer.

Sylvie attended private school in Lebanon and got her degree at St. Joseph University in Beirut. While at school she participated in all kinds of sports; now doesn't have the time. She loves to swim, but "I must tell you, the ocean here is very cold for me."

Travel is a special interest too. She has been in France, Great Britain, Belgium, and all through Syria in the middle east. A slim, very pretty girl with dark curling hair and a warm smile, she will be hosted during her stay here by Rotarians and their wives: the John Downings, the Leo Heffernans, the Leo Martins, the Al Packards and the Kai Suhrs.

Sylvie's host families have heard nothing of her since the war in the Middle East.

The Furbish Twins

July 5, 1972

AT 2:30 A.M. LIGHTS come on in the Furbish house on the Sea Road in Kennebunk. The twins, Edith and Ethel, have started their day.

They do their chores: feed the cats, feed the hens. Then they do a bit of housework, prepare breakfast. At 5:00 A.M. the paper arrives. It has to be read thoroughly ("We don't like to hurry."). Then, like as not, Miss Edith goes to "the hill" (Summer Street) where on certain days she helps folks with their housecleaning. In any case, at 5:50 A.M. she drives her sister to "the mill," Kesslen Shoe Company, where Miss Ethel has been on the payroll for thirty-eight years. When their day is done, they eat soup or crackers and milk and go to bed.

The twins were born in 1888. Their birthday this month is their eighty-fourth. Each is little more than five feet tall. Miss Edith weighs eighty-five pounds, Miss Ethel ninety-five. "When we were little, Edith got an English sovereign for gaining weight. She's got it on now. It belonged to Uncle John Elwell. He was strangled and robbed in a Salt Lake City hotel. They got the money and government bonds he had on him but his watch and gold sovereign were sent back to our mother."

The land the twins care for around their house is fifteen acres, eight of them woodland; included is a three-quarter-acre vegetable garden. To help them they have a tractor, a roto-tiller, a lawn mower and a pick-up truck—all of which they operate themselves.

Recently they sold their 1941 Dodge pick-up truck to buy a bright blue 1972 Datsun. The sisters get their new purchase out of the shed to show us. Their movements are quick, birdlike. The camera won't be able to capture them, nor the brightness of their blue eyes, nor probably even the grin-quirk at the corners of their mouths.

We say, "Miss Edith, you're the one who's going to be driving it; how about your getting back into the driver's seat?" Miss Edith hops like a chickadee into the driver's seat.

"Miss Ethel, would you get into the back?" Miss Ethel lets down the tailgate, leaps up and in. We focus the camera and shoot.

Miss Ethel used to drive but Miss Edith has sort of fallen sole heir to that job. The truck isn't the only vehicle Miss Edith maneuvers. There's her car too. She uses that to chauffeur Miss Ethel to her work and to drive herself to her own work.

Either sister, though, mounts the tractor that waits in the barn for the spring plowing of their three-quarter-acre vegetable garden.

And both operate the roto-tiller that waits beside the tractor. Well, we hear you thinking, what's so great about that? Lots of people do it. But how many are twins, I answer? And how many were born just twenty-three years after the end of the Civil War?

Like the stray cats the sisters harbor, their hens are pets. Or, as the twins call them, pensioners. "They just live till they get tired and die." Grain is pretty high these days so Miss Ethel puts leaves in the pen in the fall. "They're returned to the earth. The hens take care of them. I sprinkle oats and they scratch all the more. It's all worked over so's you wouldn't know there was any leaves there at all."

In the fall Miss Ethel piles leaves in the pick-up truck and takes them down behind the house to the woodland. From the garden the twins harvest fruits and vegetables to put up for winter. They aim to hold on as long as they can to their house and their rolling land with its trees and flowers and vegetable garden. "We don't want," they say as firmly as their chirping lttle voices permit, "to look out our window and see houses going up, or gas tanks. We don't want to see a mess."

Up at two-thirty, working from pre-dawn to dusk, still the sisters bubble with fun (Miss Ethel cracks the jokes; Miss Edith laughs at them). They enjoy life. We like to imagine our forebears to have been like this.

The twins are a living part of Maine's past. They show us a way of life that is dying, and we may not see their like again.

They're gone now, of course. Miss Ethel died February 1, 1988, at one hundred, Miss Edith December 12, 1989, at a hundred and one. These two, each no bigger than a pint of ginger, had done yeoman's labor all their adult lives ("adult" started considerably younger in their day than in ours), but when I interviewed them — saw their surroundings, heard the simple story of their lives — no discontent emerged. Their work, their garden, their crackers-and-milk supper, their interest in the daily paper formed a round of activity that filled their days. And they had fun. Pleasure shone in their faces, a proud pleasure, when they brought out their new pick-up ("Yeah," a local citizen said to me later, "the Furbish twins traded again, regular every thirty years"). As I watched them jump into that shiny blue Datsun – they were eighty-four at the time – I knew that the picture I'd taken of them, framed by their old house, the shed, the well-kept lawn, with their garden in the background, would be with me the rest of my life. The Furbish twins. Will we ever see their like again? No, we probably never will.

Hassina M'Hamsadji

October 4, 1972

HASSINA M'HAMSADJI was a far cry from those Arabian ancestors of hers, swathed in black, who were required by law to cover their faces from public view. Sans veil – in slacks, sweater, sandals, and bangle bracelet – she was driven to a *Star* interview by Phyllis Suhr. The Kai Suhrs are the last in this summer's series of host families in Rotary's Experiment in International Living program for the twenty-two-year-old Algerian girl before she flies home.

Adapting to the American way of life has been no problem for Hassina because she had taught French for a year in England and "I got used to it in easy stages." But she is still struck by the lack of poverty here. "You may have it but I have not seen it."

Algeria, now a socialist country and slowly emerging from poverty, has been free of French control for only ten years. The last part of her country's seven-year-war for freedom was spent by Hassina in a boarding school in Algiers. (For lack of village schools, children living outside the capital who wanted an education had to attend boarding schools.) She was one of a small minority – 50 Arabian girls as against 400 French – in a school run by a pro-French headmistress. On a night when a nearby hospital was bombed by the French, the windows of the school were blown in. "From then on the Algerian girls and the French girls were kept separate and we slept with knives under our pillows."

Later, in a free Algeria, her major at the university was Anglo-American studies. "I learned something about everything in that field. I even did a whole year of Old- and Middle-English language and literature. It gave me a better understanding of modern English." Algeria is education-minded. "We are on our way to becoming a highly literate country." A family with more than four children (Hassina's is "average — seven children") is given an education grant for the lower schools. College is free. During Hassina's first college year, in 1967-68, all of Algeria could list only 8,000 students. Now, four years later, it boasts 30,000. "A college education should be available," believes Hassina, "to everyone in the world if he wants it."

Arabian women are often said to have the world's most beautiful eyes, and behind Hassina's is a brain besides. She is working on her doctorate — a comparison of the writings of her countryman, Mohamed Dib, with our John Dos Passos, especially of the trilogies each wrote about his own country. The doctorate is pursued outside the hours demanded by her full-time job as translator for the National Oil Company. Her aim is to teach.

How about us? Does she approve of our mechanized society? Her brown eyes grow thoughtful. "Americans," she says, "seem to do everything so quickly. Their cans and packages! At home if we want dinner by eight we start cooking at six. Here people start at seven thirty." A smile softens her next statement. "I think you have lost something of natural taste. I think if I lived as you do all the time I would get tired of it. Here everybody is in a rush. At home we're relaxed."

But her visit to Maine, she says, has been a wonderful experience. "You must surely have one of the most beautiful states. Such different landscapes — flat, hills, lakes, rivers, ocean — all in one state. And so much green! This time at home everything is all burnt up."

After answering a question about her hobbies —"I like volley ball and swimming, but my real hobby is meeting people and getting to know them" — we drove Hassina back to the Suhrs. Our last glimpse of her was on their steps. She was waving. Her arms were bare, her legs free in their slacks. Her pretty, smiling face was in full view.

How envious must be the ghosts of her ancestors.

Hassina decided not to return to Algeria but to marry a "Mainer" instead, named Michael Taylor. They live in Lyman with daughter Jamila, thirteen. Hassina teaches French at Kennebunk High School. She has returned to Algeria five times since her visit to Kennebunk in 1972 but likes Maine and her life here too much to return permanently.

Saint Ginny

February 14, 1973

ONCE I SAID I thought of her as a modern, feminine counterpart of Jesus Christ. I hadn't meant to be profane. Divinity aside, she had Christly qualities: gentleness; compassion; generosity; forgiveness; tolerance; a need to champion the weak; an ability to feel no hate, only sorrow. (She had something else that Jesus may have had but that the Bible does not credit him with – humor.)

Those who knew Virginia Mann will appreciate that I met her in a most appropriate way. One day, sixteen years ago, we passed on the steps of the Kennebunk Post Office and she knelt to stroke my dog. (Ginny didn't pat dogs; she caressed them.) She looked up at me wistfully. "How I'd love to have a dog."

"Why don't you?" I asked. Her husband, it seemed, didn't care for dogs. Besides, he had become blind, and a dog underfoot would be hazardous.

In time her husband died. Not long afterward Ginny drove to the Biddeford pound. She came home with two dogs. There may have been a cat too – I forget. In any case it wasn't long before there were not only one cat but two, then a stream of them. And a stream of dogs.

Ginny felt bad that the world is as it is. People's inhumanity to each other and to animals nearly killed her. She must have cried in private, but I knew her to cry only once. When the cancer made it necessary for her to prepare to enter a Portland hospital, she took her animals to be destroyed – they were old, and who would want an old mongrel? She cuddled each dog, each cat, while the vet inserted the needle. It would have been easier to save herself this agony, but she had to know that they felt her hand as they died. (Did someone do as much for you, Ginny?)

All her animals were strays. She could not resist a stray. She found it impossible, in fact, to resist any need, spoken or unspoken, of human or animal. Her pocketbook was as open as her heart, though not so full. Once I asked her how she fared financially. The question happened to come up right after her lawyer—who must have noted her Spartan way of life—had told her she could "dip into capital and still have enough to see her through." For many people, dipping into capital is as obscene as walking nude down Main Street. Ginny was jubilant. She feared being a care to anyone as she grew older, but her lawyer had given her the green light to go on spending for people and animals and charity, and especially for the animal shelter in West Kennebunk that she had helped found.

Who knows much of Ginny's past? Not I. She almost never talked about herself. Bits and pieces trickled out to me, and no doubt to others, but only by accident. She was educated; she'd attended Vassar. She had a beautiful and talented sister, an actress. Ginny herself was not pretty, and an operation on her throat had left her voice rasping, reedy. But she'd been married twice. Once she gave me a drawing of a horse. It had been done with bold strokes; it was the essence of Horse. The artist was a Polish cavalry officer, and he had given his drawing to Ginny. He was dead now, she said. I suspected romance. There must have been other discerning men, besides the two husbands, who had seen the character-beauty behind her thin, long face and rather sharp features.

Last September she gave me slippers she'd crocheted while she'd been in Webber Hospital. And when a friend called me this afternoon—I was in New York—to tell me Ginny had died, my first thought, strangely, was of the slippers. I won't wear those slippers, I thought. That way I'll always have something Ginny's hands had worked.

Now I'm thinking that I will wear them, wear them out. There's something better than keeping mementos of the dead. When I do any of those things that made Ginny what she was—when I rescue a stray, or champion a lost cause, or make a gift that means a sacrifice, or try to ease someone's trouble (it won't be often; I'm no Ginny), or leave my body, as she did, for medical research—her spirit will be close. Closer than the slippers on my feet.

We can't tell of course what continued rivers of compassion Ginny would have directed toward people and animals had she lived. We know that she'd have kept on being kind and helpful to distressed humans and would always have picked up strays, assuring that they found love, food, and shelter somewhere — in her own home or in whatever refuge she could find for them. Today life would have been easier for her physically and emotionally. Due in great part to her efforts, added to those of other animal-caring persons, the home of Eldora Boston (another Ginny) in West Kennebunk has expanded into a large shelter. Ginny was one of the founders of the *Animal Welfare Society, Inc.*, complete with on-call medical and surgical help, runs, training classes, and plenty of a quality found missing in too many homes — love. There is even a pet laundromat where owners may themselves clean and groom their four-footed friends. Damaged strays are cured, if possible, and given, after careful scrutiny of the applicant, to those wanting a dog or cat. If the animal is too far gone, it is painlessly put to sleep. In a way this is one memorial to Ginny. A more specific one came in the form of a clinic, built after Ginny's death by Dr. Frank Vigue, the veterinarian to whom Ginny took animals she had rescued from abuse, neglect, or starvation. He named the building *The Mann Memorial Clinic For Animals.*

Acupuncture

August 1, 1973

IT WAS A STRANGE setting for acupuncture. (What had I expected? A pagoda? Temple bells?) It was the waiting room of a pediatrician, full of toys and children's books and a rocking horse by the picture window that looked out on trees and flowers of North Windham, Maine.

Dr. Margaret Millard is, first and foremost, a pediatrician. Because she has an extraordinary interest in the relief of pain she has taken up acupuncture as a "hobby," and I was there on a suggestion from Shirley Harrison (ESP columnist for the *Star*) that the hobby might make a story

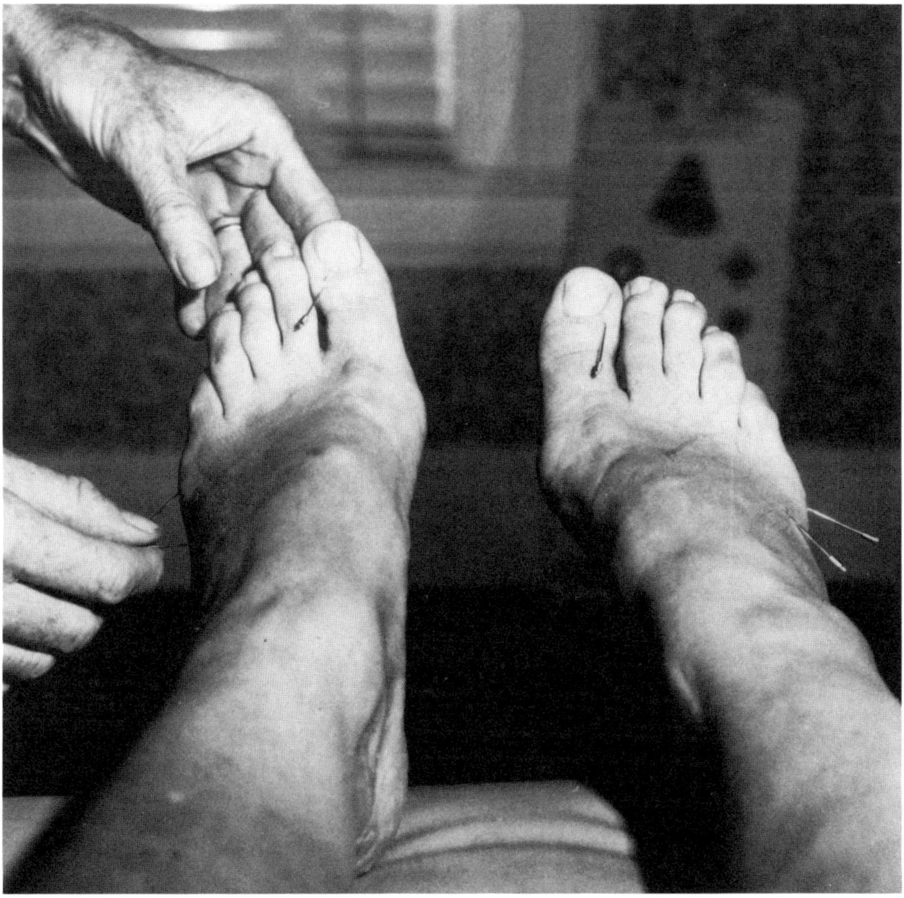

Portrait of the author by the author

for the paper, especially since, as far as can be discovered, Dr. Millard is the only physician in Maine to practice it. Shirley herself had recently undergone acupuncture by Dr. Millard. "It didn't hurt a bit," she told me. "You take a deep breath and exhale. While you're exhaling she jabs the needles in. It's not painful. Just a tiny, sharp bee-sting feeling. Not half as bad as a hypodermic needle. I just sat back and relaxed and enjoyed it," Shirley went on in her soft, confiding voice. "I said to Margaret (the doctor is her friend as well), 'You know, that feels sort of good. Sort of comforting.' The only sensation was a tingling feeling down the side of each leg [the needles were inserted in the inside of her thighs]."

As I sat now in the pediatrician's office, the last child patient had taken a last ride on the rocking horse, the last struggling mother had gone out the door, and I was next.

An amazingly young-looking woman appeared, to usher me into the examining room. Her hair, auburn with red glints, was cut short, her eyes blue, direct. She told me to undress and gave me a robe that was just a ruffle away from a hospital johnny.

"Let's kill two birds with one stone," she said briskly (unfortunate remark, I thought). "Is there anything physically wrong with you? You're here to do a story on acupuncture but I could give you a treatment at the same time."

I told her I have migraine-type headaches (pain and nausea but without the flashing lights associated with migraine). "What emotion do you feel most intensely?" she asked. "Hate? Fear? Grief?" I said, "Anxiety."

She got out her box of needles. They are small and lie in cotton batting in a box roughly four by two inches. They are silver and gold. "The gold are for sedation," she said. "The silver are tonifying." With red ink she marked two red spots on the outer edges of my feet and one on the inner big toe just below the nail root, one at the base of the big toe and one between and at the bases of the little and next toes. Red spots were then made at corresponding points on my hands. Next she drew the needles from the box.

This, I thought, was the moment of truth. Would they be painless, as Shirley had said? Would I feel like a pincushion? A stuck pig? An Indian fakir?

The needles did indeed feel like only the tiniest of bee stings, the pain over almost before felt. Although I was immobile on the table, one needle fell out of my hand. I called. Dr. Millard returned, reinserted it, and left again. I did not experience Shirley's "comforting" or "tingling" feeling.

At the end of twenty minutes the doctor came back. "Take a deep breath," she ordered. "Now exhale." On the expelled breaths she removed the needles. "Now relax for twenty minutes."

At the end of twenty minutes I got up and dressed. My acupuncture was over. (It was done nearly two weeks ago. I have not had a headache since, but I rarely have more than one or two a month anyway. I am waiting.)

Dr. Margaret Millard can't be as young as she looks because her oldest child is twenty-nine. She has five others, ranging in age down to ten. She is a pediatrician, rather than any of the other specialties she is equipped to practice — anesthesiology and obstetrics as well as general practice — because it gives her more time with her family. (While my acupuncture was in process, once she answered her phone: "Yes? Oh, darling! I'm *so* sorry. It's a shame. I'll be home very soon." She hung up. "That was my ten-year-old," she said. "She's been nursing along a bird she rescued last week. It just died. She's crying." Earlier, Dr. Millard had mentioned that she and her husband and daughter — the ten-year-old is the only child left at home — had taken a camping-canoe trip at Moosehead the previous weekend. She does not neglect her family for her practice.

She was born in the West Indies ("Oh, do you have to write about me? Let's just talk about acupuncture.") of a Canadian mother and British father. Her parents disapproved of the native schools of that time so her father taught her to read by the time she was four and a "black girl came in daily to teach arithmetic for an hour." When she was eleven she and her sister were sent to England where they were educated and where Margaret got her medical training — and a husband.

She had been practicing medicine for four years when her chemist mate was given a research grant at Amherst College. "He was a bright, young Ph.D. He solved a chemical problem over here that nobody else could crack." Later the Millards decided to become American citizens, partly so Margaret could resume her practice of medicine in this country. "We went to Durham, New Hampshire. My husband taught at UNH in the chemistry department and I became a general practitioner." They moved to Maine fifteen years ago.

Now, with an obvious perking-up of interest on Dr. Millard's part, the talk turned to acupuncture. As an anesthesiologist, she said, she became interested in ways that pain might be relieved, and when news of acupuncture surfaced (at the time of *The New York Times*'s James Reston's appendectomy under acupuncture during a visit to China), she began a serious study of this method. Learning of a course in it in Vienna for physicians by famed neurosurgeon Dr. Bischko, she enplaned as soon as possible — only six physicians are accepted for the course at one time.

Along with its techniques, Dr. Millard learned something of its history.

It may have been practiced before recorded history. A patient of mine was treated by an acupuncteur whose family has been doing it for forty generations. The oldest records are found on bone etchings of 1600 B.C. The Ebers papyrus of 1550 B.C. — the oldest Egyptian medical treatise — seems to refer to a book on the subject of "vessels," which probably were the acupuncture meridians (a back-up system for the autonomic nervous system). The Bantu of Africa commonly scratch certain parts of the body to cure disease.

To the clinic run by Dr. Bischko in Vienna in cooperation with the University of Vienna, " . . . come the arthritics, the deaf, the hypertensives, those who have had headaches for years, alcoholics and drug addicts, sufferers from trigeminal neuralgia, cerebral palsy, asthma, impotence, depression . . . " They come once a week for ten treatments. With insertion of the needles are prescribed changes in the patient's living habits: restriction of sugar (considered by acupuncteurs as very dangerous if used to excess), breathing exercises, etc.

The success of acupuncture on the individual is determined strongly by racial factors. As some people are more susceptible to drugs than others, certain races are more affected by acupuncture. It's been found that Scandinavians are the most difficult to treat, Jews the most responsive. But even the Scandinavians will respond eventually if the treatment is prolonged.

Dr. Millard still adheres to anesthesia in surgery. "It's so safe. Why use a method that's still only experimental? Acupuncture anesthesia began being used in China only a few years ago and is used more in the West for partial pain relief and relaxation in dentistry and childbirth." She feels a more reliable use of acupuncture is for postoperative pain. "The needles are left in place after an operation and when the dressings are changed the patient himself can twirl them [needles are "twisted" only for alleviation of pain, not in curative treatment] which prevents pain impulses from reaching the brain."

I asked Dr. Millard if the principle of alleviation of pain by acupuncture was that of counter-irritant. She shook her head. Neither, she said, did it have anything to do with favorable rapport between doctor and patient. You can hate your doctor and still respond to this acupuncture treatment.

No one really knows how acupuncture works. "We only know that it can do no harm and often appears to do a great deal of good. What," Dr. Millard asks, "are these 'reservoirs of energy'? Can energy really be pulled out of them to save a dying person? How can treatment of cats, before subjecting them to surgical shock, save their lives? (The treated cat survived, those untreated did not.) How can deafness be cured, especially nerve deafness? Why should a needle in the wrist cure insomnia?

"I don't pretend to have mastered the subject—I feel I won't live long enough to master it. I do, however, receive great personal satisfaction in curing my husband's bursitis or headaches in half an hour without drugs.

"The highest art of an acupuncteur," she finishes, "lies in preventive medicine, and now I can treat ailments before they become chronic . . . "

As I left, Dr. Millard said, "Please don't write about me, just about acupuncture. What I've told you about myself was only conversation."

Forgive me, Margaret Millard. Those needles weren't inserted in me by air. It's my belief that people will be interested in who belongs to the hands that did it.

Margaret Millard has retired with her husband to the Cotswolds in England, land of her British father and her schooling and medical education. As could be expected, this dynamic woman does not consider retirement a time to loll back and ponder the past. Just before her seventieth birthday she received a theatre degree (*summa cum laude*) which qualified her for all the ramifications of that demanding art—scene sets, mask, mime, makeup, and so on. Why theatre? "Why not? It encompasses everything . . . you're dealing with emotions. You learn body dynamics. You're dealing with the most interesting parts of human history: the Golden Age of Greece, the Renaissance, the Elizabethan Age. There was a core curriculum outside my major," she went on, "so I took philosophy, body language, anthropology, English Lit and English I, Spanish, Astronomy, Astronomy Lab, Photography, History of Music, History of Art, and History of Latin America. I loved it all!" Plus, "I'd like to do some storytelling. I'm very interested in Irish mythology and Celtic folklore. I predict a growing interest in storytelling in years to come."

She has given up medicine as a career but has agreed to become a consultant for a group that helps "women *before* they get pregnant." She believes in holistic medicine, has practiced it at times. " . . . You put the onus for recovery on the patient and only intervene when it's necessary. If people want a sleeping pill, you teach them instead how to relax, and adds, "Of course, if they need them, I prescribe them."

She has no specific information on increase of acupuncturists in Maine. At the time of her departure she knew of only two in Portland. (The *Portland Red* directory, covering Cumberland, Knox, Lincoln, Sagadahoc, and York counties, lists several groups of acupuncture clinics and associates as well as two individual acupuncturists. At last count there were twenty-five acupuncturists in Maine.)

Cliffhanger: The end of the story on *Maine's First Acupuncturist* had me waiting for the results of Dr. Millard's six treatments for relief of migraine. Nearly two decades now have passed without recurrence—not only of migraines but of headaches as well.

ESP Steers Searchers

Undated

EDITOR'S NOTE: Herb and Bev Brooks of Wells are down somewhere in the plane they took off in from Rochester, N.H., on September 13. All attempts to locate them have failed and the families have called on the services of Mrs. Shirley Harrison of Bar Mills, Maine, known locally and increasingly far afield for her extra-sensory perception. The *Star* sent a reporter to interview Mrs. Harrison. While she is willing for her prognostications to be made public, she defers to the family who prefer to divulge later what Mrs. Harrison has told them. Suffice to say, search planes are waiting till fog lifts to comb the area where Mrs. Harrison believes the Brookses to be.

What manner of place would she live in? We knew what Shirley Harrison looked like because we had heard her talk on extra-sensory perception (ESP), although we had not, as had so many others, seen her on TV.

We knew too that she had six children. They would be very young because she appeared to be not more than in her early thirties. A woman with the gift of ESP might live in a sombre, shuttered house. Her children might have the closed-in look of those left over-much to their own devices by a mother apart in a mystical world of her own.

We reached Salmon Falls and identified the white house by its For Sale sign. We had been told on the phone that the Harrisons were moving and we thought, approaching the driveway, that only a woman of inner peace would allow this interruption to her packing. At the end of the driveway a cat and a kitten stretched at our intrusion and flexed ominous claws. Beyond, in the barn dusk, a white horse glimmered like a birch in moonlight. Elms and maples threw a glitter of shadow on the house. Then we saw two small blond heads pop up at either end of a culvert. They belonged to the four-and-a-half-year-old Harrison twins, Michael and Eric, who were hard at work filling the culvert with rocks (discovered at this by their mother, they were scolded soundly). Shirley Harrison opened the door and the fragrance of fresh-baked cookies drifted out. It was all as far from what we had imagined as Shirley Temple is from Dracula.

This Shirley came from Island Falls, Maine. She has always lived in Maine except for a while in Pennsylvania after her marriage to Walter Harrison, now a representative for Suburban Propane Gas Corporation. Their six children range from four and a half to twenty-two. Unless she was a child bride, this would make her at least in her late thirties. The oldest child is Mrs. Goodwin Hannaford of Hollis. Margaret, seventeen, is a high school senior just back from Denmark where she was a foreign exchange student. Mark is a high school freshman, George in third grade, and the twins attend the school of (juvenile) hard knocks. There was a boy, dead in infancy, who would have been twenty-three.

The twins fought and made up and cried and begged for cookies and began great projects and abandoned them and were scolded and loved — all in the hour we were there. "Do the children interfere with your concentration?" we asked Shirley.

"No, I'm conditioned to confusion. If I'm asked to do anything serious, I try to take time out to concentrate. Otherwise, I just let things come as they will."

She gave the boy in Ft. Fairfield, for example,, who disappeared the day after Christmas last year, ten minutes of thought in the back of her car one day and suggested to the authorities that they look for him "near

Cheney's place." She had never been in Ft. Fairfield and the name Cheney meant nothing to her, but a vague something (she cannot describe these messages) had come to her that the boy died a violent death in water under a log so heavy it would require dynamite to free him. "I made the mistake of interpreting 'water' as 'river,'" she said, "and when they couldn't find him in the river they gave up the search. Three months later he was found in a swamp pinned under a 700-pound tree stump, about an eighth of a mile from Cheney's Grove."

"Why didn't they pursue the search around Cheney's Grove?" we asked. "You'd said Cheney's Place, but that was close enough."

"I think they didn't believe in ESP. They're not apt to in rural areas. It's looked on more as a superstition. Cities have more faith in it." She brought out a newspaper article on John J. Cronin, retired Commander of the N.Y. Police Missing Persons Bureau. "I believe," Cronin had said, "that it (ESP) may contribute to the solutions of many crimes in the future. Who am I to disagree with many of the world's top scientists – scientists who have advanced the theory that there are persons with the ability to perceive a dimension of truth beyond the reach of the five senses?" And he went on to tell of two famous cases where ESP had dredged up important information: Judge Crater's disappearance and the murder of Samuel Sheppard's wife.

One of the strangest things that happen is the poems that pop full-blown into Shirley's head. She is not a poet, but listen to what came to her on the day of Kennedy's funeral:

The patient earth stirs, sighs and returns
once more to sleep.
She does not hear the muffled drums, the marching
feet that mark the measure of this day's pain.
This that is, was, and will be again.
In all the tomorrows beyond the reach of time
The drifting wind will carry the sounds of grief
to the far hills
And the earth shall sleep.

Here's another:

I, cast down by priests and hooded nuns,
Banned, shunned and craven,
Did flee and hide.

Best leave and be no more
Than this bleak life I lead.
Land, home and kin denied
Best dead am I.

This, said a professor of English at Columbia University, sounded like a Rossetti poem. Shirley asked him to locate it—she wants her "messages" checked where possible—and the professor tried but failed. If you readers have any clues to these poems, please let us know.

A doctor, interested in ESP, suggested that she send her experiences to Dr. and Mrs. Rine at Duke University in North Carolina. The Rines, experimenting in ESP for many years, referred her for testing to William G. Rowe of the Psychical Research Foundation at Duke. There, Shirley underwent card tests, called "Token Object Matching," and Mr. Rowe came to Maine to test her under home conditions. In November she will go to Duke again for more tests. The Foundation experiments in many different ways, attempting to solve scientifically this mystery that was once at best termed Second Sight and at its worst saw witches burned at the stake.

"Do you ever feel different from other people?" With some diffidence we asked the question of this obviously normal woman in her normal home, who kept leaving the interview to attend to a crying child, a hungry child, or just a child who wanted to put its arms around its mother.

"No. My mother was a school teacher. She was used to children and she never made anything of it. I'd tell her that So-and-So would be calling that afternoon and what she would talk about. I'd tell her that a letter from grandmother would come tomorrow and what it would say. Mother would just take it all for granted." But for a long time, during the business of growing up, getting married, and having seven children, there was no time to work with her ESP. Suddenly it began again.

One summer, when she and her family were at their cottage at the lake, she decided for no reason she was aware of to return home two weeks earlier than planned. At 2:00 A.M. the morning of the day they were to leave she woke her husband. "Get the children up," she told him. "We've got to leave at once." Arriving home, they learned that a violent wind storm had commenced about dawn at the lake and toppled two trees onto their cottage, crushing it. "It wasn't a compulsion or a message, only an impulse," she said to us. "There was no hint of a storm brewing when we left. Why did this come to me? I just don't know."

Another time she and her husband had reached Boston by train on their way to Philadelphia. She felt suddenly they should change to a bus. "I didn't know why I had this urge. I hate buses!" In Philadelphia they learned that the train they would have taken was derailed in Rhode Island and several people were hurt.

In experimental vein, Shirley has several times told surgeons what they will find when they operate. She is told only that surgery is going to be performed. She will know nothing about the patient, not even the sex, but she is able to tell in detail what the operation will reveal.

She has also held a wire in her hands and without any clues has said accurately that it came from the Berlin Wall.

But these are in the manner of tricks, to prove her highly developed extra-sensory perception. "Everyone has it," she claims, "some more than others, but the lives of most people are such that it cannot develop." She wants to contribute to the research going on in the field of ESP. To this end, she would like a degree in psychology so she can approach it scientifically. This is just a dream now, though. She must continue to flush twins out of culverts, feed ravenous children, and tend to all the physical and emotional wounds that children magnetize.

In the meantime, her few moments of quiet concentration continue to yield things beyond her range of experience. "Everything we know," she said, "comes from a memory pattern." She picked up an envelope. "I know this is an envelope because I learned once what an envelope is. It is part of my accumulated experience." But it is what is beyond the range of memory experience that constitutes paranormal knowledge, and its source is not yet known.

If it is ever discovered, it will be in great part due to people like Shirley Harrison who have braved skepticism and given freely of their mystical experiences to the world.

A friend of Shirley Harrison reports that she died "painfully but quickly" of liver cancer. The friend saw her on May 5, 1987, three days before her death at home. "She knew it was imminent," the friend reported. "I said to her, 'I'll miss you very much,' and Shirley answered, 'I will try to get through, you know [referring to their shared belief in the possibility of life after death], but it's very difficult. It's like being in a phone booth and trying to make someone outside hear you. I don't know if I'll be able to or not.'

"The day after she died," the friend went on, "at exactly the same hour, her daughter heard a loud knocking at the door, but when she opened it no one was there. She felt it was her mother."

On the day of interview with Shirley, she had informed us that three of her six living children had extrasensory perception, the others not. Shirley believed that all persons are born with extrasensory perception. Some will develop it—as she seemed to have done unconsciously or consciously in the growing process—while others are unable to, or prefer to negate it, having fear of learning what the future holds.

3

Artists and Craftsmen

Jean and Bob Moshimer, a long-standing and richly hued partnership / Photo by Nancy Ames, 1991

The Happy Hooker

July 2, 1969

BEHIND A SIMPLE sign, "Home of Craftsman Hooked Rug Patterns," on North Street in Kennebunkport is a story of romance, of an ocean crossed, and of a new career begun at a time when most of us feel too entrenched in the old to start afresh.

When Joan (Mrs. Robert) Moshimer was a little girl in New Zealand, her dreams of what her life would be probably never included going to a new land and settling in a small Maine seaport where she would run a business with her husband. But then she didn't know Bob Moshimer from Portland, Maine. After two years of fighting with the 43rd Infantry Division in the South Pacific, Bob was sent to New Zealand in 1944 for a rest. And now in a barn in Kennebunkport he smiled down at his wife while they posed for the *Star*. "We met in March," he said, "got officially engaged in June, and were married on D-Day in August." Joan has seen her family only once since then. "I took the children back seven years ago. And—do you know?—I was homesick for Maine!"

She had been a commercial artist in New Zealand. Arriving in Maine, she did fashion design for advertising agencies and for Peck's in Lewiston. "But when I saw hooked rugs, it was the beginning of the end." She not only learned the craft with characteristic thoroughness, she began teaching it; and the Associated Press, intrigued that someone from New Zealand was instructing in hooking in an area that in Colonial times was a hotbed of hookery, did a story on her. She has given up regular teaching but will take on a class for a week this month in North Carolina, will talk at a "Hooking Bee" at the Eastern States Exposition and will take part again this year in Jordan Marsh's "Fabricana," which features her work.

What is the history of this art of poking through burlap, strips of ofttimes warmed-over cloth? "No one really knows," says Joan. "The Egyptians may have started it. Shreds of hooked materials have been found in their tombs. The early Scandinavians did it. Scottish people in Nova Scotia did it. Colonial women brought the craft over with them. They hated to throw anything away, so they took strips of old clothes and hooked rugs to cover their dirt floors. The Maritimers of eastern Canada were active hookers too."

How does she instruct someone who wants to learn the art? "First I give a demonstration. Then I furnish them with an easy design. We have kits." She picked up an attractive plastic package. "You see, the design is already stamped on burlap. Incidentally, we import our burlap from Scotland; it's of better quality. There's a rug hook in the kit and an instruction sheet and enough wool for the design. Cutters – they cut cloth into strips – aren't included but we have them for sale." The kit was $3.50. Its design, by Joan, is of chickadees on a twig laden with berries and it has been featured in *Workbasket*, a national home arts magazine.

The word "dyed" introduces husband Bob. Last fall he left thirty years of work in a Portland business to handle growing mail orders for dyes, patterns, and hooking paraphernalia. The dyes have been made in Dover-Foxcroft, Maine, by W. Cushing & Co. since the day Wainwright Cushing, a dyer in a textile mill there, came home from the Civil War with the idea that housewives might welcome small-packaged dyes for home use. Wainwright started with just one color, "Turkey Red," a popular hue with nineteenth century homespinners. It is still listed on the Cushing color chart along with ninety-four others that bear such titillating names as "Egyptian Red," "Mummy Brown," "Khaki Drab," "Nugget Gold," etc. Cushing Company, which has been bought by the Moshimers, takes Bob north about once a week.

He finds mail order the most intriguing of his new duties because of letters that pour in from throughout the world. One from the U.S. Embassy in Kuala Lampur (Malaysia) asked for all information on batik. "The funny thing about this is, batik started in Malaysia." And a nun in a leper colony in South Africa asked about Cushing dyes for her patients to work with. Bob sent her samples and a letter came back with her order. She had stirred the dye, she said, in an iron kettle over a wood fire in the back lot, feeling like a witch in her long black robe, churning a potent brew in a cauldron.

The present resurgence of hooking has been given impetus by Joan's articles in home magazines and by her handsome, illustrated catalogue, hand printed by herself. She is now "writing" (hand printing) a book, and the Moshimers will soon start a monthly newsletter for hookers or "ruggers," a term comprising both hookers and braiders. According to the Moshimers, hooking is a burgeoning craft. "People have more leisure and they want to do something with their hands. Children are taking it up, and men too. We have half a dozen inquiries a day from people wanting to start a business of their own in either dyeing or hooking."

We said to Joan, "Your rugs are beautiful, but tell us what makes a 'bad' hooked rug."

Her reply: "Every hooked rug is lovely, because so much of the person making it has gone into it."

The Happy Hooker Revisited

July 8, 1970

THIS IS A PROGRESS report on Joan and Robert Moshimer.

When the Moshimers came to Kennebunkport about a year ago, the *Star* reported the fact in its July 2, 1969, issue. It told how New Zealand-born Joan had met the American soldier who was to become her husband. How, on arriving in America, she did fashion design before immersing herself in the craft of rug hooking. And of how the Moshimers moved to the 'Port from Portland because they fell in love with a big house on North Street and thought what a wonderful studio-shop its barn would make.

Their rug-hooking business has flourished (with the help of two valuable assistants, Norma Allen and Barbara Campbell). Batik supplies have been added and the Moshimers are going even more into kits, those stuffed plastic bags that enable the hooker to hook her favorite design without the tedious work of first assembling materials and tools. There is a kit for tie dyeing that looks like a child's toy because of the marbles it contains to use in making the design. The kit also has dyes, measuring spoons, color card, enough wool for two neckties and even string to tie the wool around the marbles. All kits, of course, include complete instructions, attractively hand printed and illustrated by Joan. One of the instruction sheets is "Spot Dye for Fashion Fabrics," and the visitor is sometimes shown two lovely long evening skirts Joan whipped up recently from some of her spot-dyed fabric.

There are times when she leaves her beloved and rich-hued barn — its hanging wools and color cards and rugs making a kaleidoscope of color — and goes far afield to spread the hooking word. During the week of July 13th she will teach at the Douglas-Poole Craft School in North Carolina. On July 23rd she will speak at the Eastern States Exposition Hooking Bee in Springfield, Massachusetts, an annual engagement for her although this year dyeing rather than hooking will be her subject.

Dyeing has become an integral part of the Moshimers' craft activities. Husband Bob makes periodic trips to Dover-Foxcroft in north-central Maine where his factory produces the variety of dyes that end up in wools in the big barn on North Street.

Joan is continually coming up with new designs. One of her latest is "Apollo 11," a handsome space design that was accepted ceremoniously last spring by Governor Curtis for the State Museum. In August this enterprising woman will put on a hooked-rug show for the Kennebunkport Historical Society. The rugs will be old and local. If not enough emerge from 'Port homes, they will be imported from outside; but in an area as rich in antiquity as Kennebunkport Joan feels she will have no trouble.

A talent such as Joan's can't help being picked up by a national publication. In the April 1970 issue of *Family Circle* appeared the article "Meet Mrs. Robert Moshimer of Kennebunkport, Maine — Hooked Rugs Designed to Make Money," in the Careers-at-Home section.

And a final item in the progress report: Joan's literary agents, McIntosh & Otis of New York, say there is a need for a how-to hooked-rug book — who is better qualified to write it than Mrs. Moshimer? (And Scribner's is interested.) Hooked-rug aficionados take note.

Space is not available for a complete listing of Joan Moshimer's rug-hooking activities since the seventies. This update, therefore, is limited to only a portion of what has been published *by* her not *about* her.

About the time of our first meeting, in 1969, Joan was writing — not typing, not dictating — with her own agile fingers instructions to go into a kit on how to hook rugs, handwriting in the conviction that this method of telling how-to was more in tune with the homey quality of the craft. Then *The Complete Book of Rug Hooking* was published in 1975. In 1972 she had started publishing and editing the magazine *Rughooker, News and Views* which spread like a benign epidemic through the rug-hooking areas of the United States, Canada, England, Japan, Australia, and New Zealand. It later was renamed *Rug Hooking*, with Joan its consultant and editor. (The magazine is now being published by Stackpole Books, Harrisburg, PA.) Then came *Hooked On Cats*, a how-to book, subject matter, kittens, lions, and tigers.

Husband Bob's managerial expertise has now passed on to their son Paul who is aided by his artist-wife Pat. The family is licensed by Massachusett's Old Sturbridge Village to print an important collection of rug patterns designed by Pearl K. McGowen. It is licensed also to print the collection of Edward Sands Frost's patterns, owned by the Henry Ford Museum in Dearborn, Michigan. (Frost, incidentally, was a post Civil War Yankee peddler from Biddeford, Maine.)

We end with an editorial by Joan in *Rughooker, News and Views*: [In the beginning of launching herself in the craft] " . . . it wasn't long before I began to understand how very important this occupation [rug hooking] is to a great many people (men as well as women) in this sometimes uncaring and impersonal world. It helps us to be in touch with our true selves, to keep us on an 'even keel.'"

Joan Moshimer's Rug Hooker Studio, North Street, P.O. Box 351, Kennebunkport, ME 04046-0351.

Two York County Crafters

April 19, 1972

SAID THE WOMAN behind the desk as we passed through Nasson's library on our way into the Hildreth Gallery, "You're going to enjoy yourself. It's a great show!"

She was right. We *did* enjoy ourselves and it *is* a great show.

And the fact that the two exhibitors are York County coasters added chauvinistic lustre to the exquisitely worked pots and jars of Ogunquit's Peter Craft and the vivid or subtle but always beautiful weavings of Kennebunkport's Muriel Hart.

As a weaver Muriel Hart is five years old; as an artist she is somewhat older. Since the time she studied with Reginald Marsh at the Art Students League in New York she has been involved with some form of art—at Warner Brothers and the Walter Lantz Motion Picture Studios in California where she did scenic design and animations in their cartoon department; with her own gallery and shop in Carmel; as a free-lancer illustrating magazine articles, and in advertising and greeting card design; as a teacher of art in Carmel's elementary schools; and as a photographer.

For a year she was craft director in Germany with the Army's Special Services and craft director of her own shop for woodworking, leather working, and pottery. "I didn't know how to weave then," she says ruefully. "I wish I had. Some German donated a beautiful six-foot hand-made loom and it just sat there because nobody knew how to work it."

Her interest in weaving was born in Europe, and after she left Special Services she traveled the continent a year, visiting weaving studios. Returning to Carmel, she read omniverously about weaving, and then "I married Dan (Daniel Hart, now head of the Industrial Arts Department of Kennebunk High School) and this changed my whole life. We left California for Maine," where she heard about the Haystack Mountain School of Crafts at Deer Isle. "I studied there with Toshiko Horiuchi, one of the most marvelous people I've ever met. She's back in Japan now. Our loss. She's a Cranbrook (School of Crafts) person. That's the Harvard of craft schools."

It followed as the night the day that Muriel must have a loom of her own, so Dan made her one and she began weaving full time. Muriel has an incandescent grin. She flashes it and says, "I know I have found my niche."

She and Dan are building a studio at the Port (Kennebunkport) where she'll be teaching and exhibiting her weaving, and where "I'll welcome anyone who wants to come in and talk about weaving. I want to give people who are interested everything I know about weaving. Anyone can weave if they really want to."

The fortuitously named Peter Craft, an art teacher in the Wells school system, has lived in Ogunquit for two years since graduating from the Rhode Island School of Design with a master's degree. He was a sculptor first—his major at college—then he was drawn to pottery ("it was a gradual thing but the actual switch was abrupt"), which he considers the most fascinating form of art. "It is a constant lesson in life; you don't control everything."

Every time you open a kiln, he claims, it's like having a child. You don't know what the thing you put in is going to look like. "Potters who've worked for forty or fifty years still have that element of surprise. You can never know enough about fire and the kiln to have perfect results every time. Unless," he adds seriously, "unless you make toilet seats. Then they all come out right."

He loves small, Incan-like figures on his jars and vases. He is in fact influenced by the pre-Columbian period. "I never realized you could get that much detail in pottery." He has to keep the little figures under plastic coverings which he takes off for an hour each day to dry them. "It takes a long time. Clay shrinks when it dries, and if one part dries sooner than another the piece is going to break." Ideally he should have a sealed room with a humidifier in his studio for drying uniformly, but the expense is prohibitive, and when a man is married (to a lovely brunette pianist) and has three small boys, expense has to be considered.

Several years ago the Harts moved to Carmel, California. Muriel trained to become a docent in the Monterey Aquarium; illustrated a book, *My Neighbors in Elkhorn Slough*, about creatures of the estuary there; and at present is preparing for a trip to the Orient, ending in Hong Kong for "lots of craft-oriented visits to hill tribes making silk, jewelry, baskets. I'll go berserk as I did in India. Thai silk is a passion of mine and I aim to indulge [it] this time." This, she says, is not to be for clothing but for wall hangings, embroidered, a craft which she is now doing.

Peter Craft cannot be traced.

A Way With Wood

June 28, 1972

DAN DUSTIN AND his wife Kendall, living on the east bank of the Kennebunk River in Lower Village, are of a growing number of young people who are returning to the land and the ways of their forefathers.

Both are college graduates, Dan with a degree in industrial psychology ("that's figuring out why people aren't happy in their work"). He is a flutist in the 'Port Concert Trio, gives flute lessons and is a trained harpsichord maker.

He loves wood. Much of it he scavenges. After he has allowed it to weather in his yard he makes buttons, buckles, spoons, bowls, jigsaw puzzles, counter tops, furniture, drawer knobs, tools, doors—name it and Dan can in all probability make it. Out of his love for wood have developed convictions that he imparts in quick asides, as if in time to the pounding of nails: "I believe wood should be allowed to warp before it is joined . . . I like a piece of wood to sit until it is comfortable . . . I am forced to use antique tools because I want the beauty of my gathered wood . . . My esoteric craftsmanship is not just because I'm a nut . . . A repaired wood is more beautiful . . . Nothing is as beautiful in woodwork as a mistake corrected.

"We live in my grandmother's house. She died two years ago. Uncle Lawrence looked at the porch and said, 'That won't last the summer.' That was thirty years ago. It lasted because he kept it up. He was my first teacher in woodcraft. He does things the right way."

As their ancestors probably did, Dan and Kendall trade quite a bit: A door for the doctor, to pay for their baby's birth. ("We didn't want to pay one hundred and seventy-five dollars. That's half my life savings!") A sign for a shop that in turn will display Dan's work. Woodworking in exchange for lobsters, clams, and "birthday cakes." And like many of their peers they are not above scavenging. A half ton of coal discovered in an abandoned cellar hole. Old nails. A squash and some apples—once

"Here's one of the two widest Norway pine boards I've ever seen in Maine. A little over twenty inches, I've buried it to let it season. It will make a table top someday . . . " / Photo by the author, 1972

a dozen pumpkins — floating in the river. Old Oriental rugs from the Kennebunkport dump.

I pick up wood at dumps that people have thrown away. It's scarred and dirty. Some of it has rats' nests. I don't like to pick up driftwood and sell it. Generally speaking I have my eye on a piece of driftwood a year before I bring it home. I have hiding places on the coast. Six months ago I found a crummy piece of furniture. I took the formica off, took off some horrible tin stuff. The wood was beautiful! Then I turned it upside down in the mud to season and left it. I lost that piece. Maybe it floated off. But the work I did isn't wasted. Someone will find it, and it will be beautiful.

Dan is twenty-five, Kendall twenty-three. Elders may look at young people like the Dustins in different ways — some with envy, some askance, some perhaps don't bother to look. Dan and Kendall do not care. Dan is doing what gives him happiness. What gives it to him is the work he does with his hands. Sometimes it isn't "happy" work but only the sense of a job well done.

Like the coffin for Pat Bordage. Pat was his friend and they were business partners besides. Dan made things out of wood that Pat dived for in the Saco River. Pat drowned in that river two weeks ago. Dan worked a day and most of one night fashioning a coffin out of river wood for Pat's body. "If he could have seen it," Dan said, "he probably would have said nothing; it was his way to express gratitude in action instead of words."

Several years after the above interview the Dustins were reported to have moved to New Hampshire. It is not known if Dustin continued his work with wood.

Michael Palmer, Artist

July 26, 1972

IN A LITTLE house at Moody Beach lives a tall man who paints large paintings. Sometimes he paints small ones too, but mostly the canvases are large.

The man paints at a table on a tilted board, facing the Atlantic Ocean. The light pours full onto his face. That is the way he likes to paint.

Once his paintings were black and white. Some still are. Now, though, they are increasingly in shades of brown and in blues that fade to grey. More recently—and gingerly, as if bright color were a dangerous thing—red has begun to creep in.

Some of the people the man paints are silent people with secrets. They converse, in tones too low for you to hear, with their backs to you or in profile. They think their thoughts alone in rowboats. Ecstatic and alone they feel the fall of rain on their faces. Or they live, unseen by you, in fantasy houses of slow decay, to become, in the end, ghosts that glide through empty rooms and mount a creaking staircase.

Sometimes, though, the man's canvases burst with life. Two small boys soar in swings. One crashes through the boundary of the canvas edge; your imagination follows his upward surge. The other contorts his body to wrest from the ropes the ultimate crest. Human figures cavort on the limbs of a stripped banyan in *The Magnificent Tree,* and children chatter atop reflected pilings whose thrust is reversed in blue water.

Michael Palmer is the name of the tall man. Friendly, slow-spoken, he refuses to dramatize the act of painting, telling of his work much as a carpenter might talk about planing. No one in Michael's family painted except an uncle who, because he married young and had a family young, turned from serious to commercial art out of necessity, and who used to pay what must have been wistful visits to a small Michael, carrying to him pictures of great art cut from magazines.

Michael was neither encouraged nor discouraged to paint. His mother, loving music and art and books, may have been less concerned about her only son's trend to art than a father who had struggled out of Kentucky mountain poverty ("he's hill-billy stock, not hill-billy type") to hold rank in the U.S. Air Force and retire to high-school counseling in Louisville. "You've got to teach art to make a living at it," Michael quotes him as saying. But it was not the goal of teaching that kept Michael taking art courses wherever his family went.

Should you expect answers from an artist on why he paints the things he does? They came, from Michael: Why those wrecks of houses; houses that come through gaunt and haunted, and silvered (or coppered) by age into shingle shrouds for those who may live and die within? "Actually," Michael says drily, "in the Kentucky hills (Kentucky was where he was born on December 8th, 1942) a house like that would be lived in." Anyway, he likes houses that are "irregular. A white, well-painted house – what's there to paint?"

The children that populate his canvases?

Adult figures are harder to manipulate. "In a child, any position goes. If a child makes the design work, then I use a child. I'm not any more attached to kids than anybody else, I suppose. I certainly don't want to have any. I have enough friends with kids I can enjoy."

The reflection in still water that has become almost his signature?

"I don't know. It's fun. And it works very well as a tool, as a piece of your design material. There's one I did – after finishing it I got silly and even reflected the signature."

His colors of browns and blues?

"I like all the earth tones. Then I started using blues. Now I've just started with brighter tones here and there. That fruit stand – I stuck red in at the last minute and it brought it all together."

He works without models. He had too much of that in life class, he says. For him, to have something alive to paint from kills a piece.

Perhaps, too, no model could stand the strain. Michael gets up at 5:30 and after breakfast sits down at his work. He works through the afternoon and after dinner until he goes to bed. The past year he averaged a painting a day. The realization of this horrifies him. "That sounds terrible. I'm *not* running a mill and whacking them out." When he tires he lets it go for a while and works in his garden (he grinds up his garbage in a Waring blender to make instant compost).

It hasn't always been all work. The Air Force often makes gypsies of its personnel and Michael saw the world before he settled into the house at Moody Beach. At four he left Panama to travel with his family to posts throughout the United States. He lived in Japan for four years (some of his work has a faint Oriental cast). Then Hawaii ("my favorite place; I was old enough then to really enjoy it"). Transfer to Georgia came and Michael stayed on in Atlanta after his father's retirement. He tried to live by painting. He was poor. "It was before hippy days but I did the sort of thing hippies do. Lived in a basement apartment. Mattress on the floor." He was a professional college dropout. He had attended the Universities of Hawaii, Kentucky, and Kansas City and took art courses at all. He decided to finish college "just for the heck of it." A University of New Hampshire degree decided him on staying in the New England coastal part of the world.

He shows so far in galleries in Massachusetts, Texas, Montreal, and Washington. In York County his work has been seen at Chris Ritter's Ogunquit Gallery, the Gallatins' Kittery Point Gallery, and the Priscilla Hartley Gallery in Kennebunkport. He has given shows periodically. He is depressed after them. "I get uninspired by everything." He thought he had broken this pattern one winter in Dallas. The show was a fantastic success, sold out in three days. "I felt so good! Anxious to get home and really get to work. I got home. I sat down. Nothing!" This lasts two or three days. He feels drained, "like maybe when a woman has a baby or an architect finishes a house." Then he gets up one morning and sits down, blank, at his work table— unless he is in the middle of something big he always sits down blank—

And discovers inspiration has been born again.

Palmer has been at home with color for a long time now. His early earth-pigments are still a part of his canvas but not predominant as they once were. His scenes of lonely derelict houses on islands or by the sea carry more the feeling of places shared in remembered past. They still, though, maintain the same aura of mystery they have had since the start. His people, especially children, never seem to "pose" for him—nor in fact do they; they grow fresh out of his mind or a memory of them. Rarely do the children acknowledge his presence: they are most often at the point of darting away or too deep in thought or conversation to make him a part of their absorption.

The characters, especially of his large canvases, are often presented to the viewer as not confronting him but with their backs to him or with their heads turned from him. They are lost in thought or in a conversation whose words must not be revealed. Andrew Wyeth was inclined toward this (for example, his "Christina's World"), yet the environment of the two artists in their formative years was strikingly different and Palmer's talent is his own, in no way consciously influenced.

Palmer continues to turn out a stream of work, each painting unique; we are never faced with assembly-line quality.

To date his one-man shows number sixteen; group juried, fourteen; gallery affiliations, four; public collections, eleven; private (these are collections only of those widely notable for their acquisitions), five; publications, three. Other affiliations: owner, P.S. Galleries; president, Ogunquit Art Association, 1974-1977; Artists Equity, New York City.

The Loves Of Warren Butler

March 28, 1973

THE HOUSE WAS shrouded in mist after the day's heavy rains and the lights within made it shimmer as if it were under water, and the man coming from the house seemed to be emerging from the sea, in his green corduroy the color of certain ocean weeds, and his jacket fastened with black frog loops that in the half light resembled shells.

Entering the house with him was to step back across the years to when clipper ships winged homeward with rugs and procelains and jade, with paintings of slender mountains and carvings of ivory and sweet wood, bought by captains from shops smelling of incense or in the joss houses of China or from aristocrats down on their luck.

The dreamy mist of outside invaded the house. A red Chinese "gate of heaven" gave onto ceiling and walls dense with vines. It was a room where gold and crimson flashes of fish darted through aquatic worlds, where wicker settee and chairs and table seemed part of a wild and natural setting.

In other parts of the house, although lamps were ready, the rooms were dimly lit by the glow from hidden lights in wall niches that bore, each, a ship's model. The walls of the niches are painted: mountains rise above palm trees on the shores of a bay. Small boats tossing on angry seas point up the elegance of the model. Serene, it "sails" in prevailing winds or lies at anchor in a calm harbor.

Warren Hathaway Butler, who lives with his wife in this house at Biddeford Pool, is builder of the models. Most of the leisure hours of his eighty-four years have been spent on the ship models now in his home or on display in Peabody Museum in Salem, Massachusetts.

It is the old ships, more than his models, that Warren Butler loves. It was to add another dimension to this love that he learned the art that enables his fingers to carve minute figureheads, shape planks and the tiny pegs that join them, even to place plateware on infinitesimal tables in captains' tiny quarters. He builds his models as the early ships were built, from the first element, the backbone (a composite of keel, stem and stern post), then, at each cross section of the ship, placing the frames (ribs) from the keel to the gunwale and joining them together at deck level by the deck beams—each a process done painstakingly by hand.

The little-boy Warren, hanging around carpenters in Salem, "milked them dry of information about tools and woods." At thirteen he made his first "really good" model, of a small knock-about yawl. He made it of red oak, split and sawed from a piece of firewood, and hand-worked for it the "new spoon bow that had just come in. It looked so beautiful compared to the old cutter bow." Another early model was made from part of a mahogany counter found in his grandfather's store. "It had been there for generations. It was really cured." Now he uses mostly basswood, the American linden favored by bird carvers.

The sea and its ships are in Warren Butler's blood. He was born in Salem, and he learned to sail in the Penobscot Bay region, his favorite boat a sailing dory. (It was in Blue Hill that his sister, Katharine Butler Hathaway, some thirty years ago wrote her tender story *The Little Locksmith* about her malformed legs.) Still, Warren Butler was not to become a sailor. He went to Harvard, on to Harvard Law School, and became a member of the Massachusetts Bar, and during a year's practice in Boston discovered that although he liked the law he had developed a distaste for contention. He left and entered his mother's business, managing department stores in Salem.

As president of the American Retailers, Inc., he would be asked to survey a department store somewhere in the United States and out of this geographical glimpse would come a period of wanderings. "I have spent the night in every state in the union including Alaska [Hawaii was not yet part of the U.S.]." A self-styled hobo —"I was an amateur" — he walked the highways and byways, exchanging food and sleep for wood-cutting or similar chores. He came to know first-hand his country and its people. And when his namesake grandson left a job as cartoonist at the Pentagon to go around the world, paying his way by selling his pen-and-ink drawings, it was with his grandfather's blessing and perhaps his envy, because Warren Butler is as much a traveler as the men who sailed his beloved ships. He has seen most of the world except the Orient (ironic; that is clipper country). He dreamed of going there, of taking off on a tramp steamer to roam those fabled lands. Now he feels it is too late. (Perhaps, Warren Butler, it is better to leave some things to dreams?)

In their treasure-trove house he and his wife are content. They serve icy martinis to guests, poured from an old English pitcher into matching egg cups. Egg cups? Yes. When a M. Pechaud, a druggist of New Orleans, concocted a brandy mixed drink some years ago he served it in egg cups, the right size for his drink. The French word for egg cups is "coquetier," which became corrupted by Americans to "cocktay," which in turn became "cocktail." This is a tid-bit you might hear over a Butler martini. Then their children might be mentioned: Harriet Shreve (of Shreve, Crump and Lowe family), ethnologic assistant curator of the Peabody Museum; Elizabeth Frothingham, now in Paris where her husband is opening a Paris branch of the Chemical Trust Company; Jonathan, who teaches and helps administrate at a community college in Beverly, Massachusetts. The children visit and bring their children ("We have eight grandchildren — I think."). And one great-granddaughter.

There could be mention too, over cocktails, of Mrs. Butler's cooking. "Her scallop stew — why, people write for her recipe from all over the world." Mrs. Butler scowls and grumbles, "I hate cooking. Refuse to do it." And breaks into a laugh.

And so they live. Warren Butler writes poetry, nurtures his plants, his vines and his goldfish, holds conversations with a fat dachsund and a black cat. And makes his models.

" . . . Ah but a man's reach should exceed his grasp," says the poet. "Or what's a heaven for?" Warren Butler is still reaching beyond the perfection that he seems already to have grasped.

. . . There was a light on the water that was not the light of the moon or the stars or the dawn,

(Though stars were out after storm)
That diffused and gleamed along all the edges of the clouds
In that strange dark world: as it descended
Upon the slow, moving waters, tumultuous no longer,
It seemed as if they had themselves become luminous,
Borrowing no light from either the sun or the moon or the stars.
It burnished her decks to silver (though her sides were black)
And fell along the delicate network of her shrouds . . . *

Warren Butler had it all — a lovely wife, children and grandchildren, a beautiful home on Maine's coast, an army of friends, and an unsurpassed talent for carving exquisite models of old sailing ships, a lifetime hobby to which he was devoting his retirement years.

On January 22, 1974, preparing for a visit from members of his family, he went to his living room, the German mug in his hand filled with gasoline intended for a smoldering fire. Reaching the fireplace he poured the mug's contents directly onto the logs. The instant explosion shot flames at him, igniting his clothing. The housemaid, hearing the burst, rushed to the living room and saw "an object" on the floor, engulfed in fire.

Warren Butler was already dead.

*An excerpt from "The Reuben & Martha," by Warren H. Butler, in his book *Poems*.

4

Concerned Citizens

Indifference now . . . in two weeks love? / Photo by the author, 1968

Friendly Town

August 3, 1966

IT'S BACK TO ITS old tricks again—that wayward bus that brings New York Fresh Air children to Kennebunk. For two years it's been on time. This year, because the train it met from New York was late, the bus arrived at Kennebunk last Wednesday forty-five minutes late. It's hard on waiting hosts— the town hall steps grow no softer with time—but good for the *Star* because it gave time for a little interviewing.

Many "repeats" were on hand, families who year after year take these children out of the sweltering city and give them two weeks or more of fresh air and fun. There were also several "first-time" families, many from outside the Kennebunks.

The wives of brothers Robert and Richard Anderson were there from Dayton, both first-timers. The two families already own eight children between them and each family is entertaining two Fresh Airs who are going to be taking the Red Cross swimming course in Arundel while they're here.

Mrs. Harold Bruns, neighbor to the Andersons, has six of her own and is taking two visitors. "I'm a bear for punishment," she laughed.

Mrs. Marshalyne Pullen, sitting on the town hall steps with sons Ricky and Skipper, is taking one boy. Would that all interviewees were as loquacious as Skipper, aged six! "My mommy was named Smith first," he informed us immediately. "She got married to my daddy. His name is Raymond. My mommy's thirty years old. My dad's thirty-three. I'm going to school next year for the first time." We finally had to leave this reporter's dream. "I'm going to swimming school next year too," he called after us.

We stopped a moment with the John Downings, three years old as hosts. "Wilton coming again this year?" we asked. "Oh, yes," said John. "He'll probably be out in the boat fifteen minutes after he gets here." John had Susan, four, by the hand. Wife Nancy held the baby. "We've got a bike lined up for him," Nancy said. "Wiltie wrote us last winter, 'I love you all.' Wasn't that nice?"

Dr. and Mrs. Robert Livonia of Kezar Falls are new hosts. He was born in Paris, Maine, but served his osteopathic internship in Bangor and has practiced in Kezar Falls five years. The family likes to ski, one reason they settled here. "Charley likes to ski too," the doctor said, smiling down at his three-year-old son, "but last year he took off his skis all the time and drank hot chocolate at the lodge." Were there other Fresh Air hosts from Kezar Falls? "Not yet," the doctor said, "but this is a tremendous thing. Maybe others up there will do it next year."

When the bus arrived, one of Virginia Mann's two Fresh Air boys jumped off, then gazed up at Frank Stevens, Kennebunk's police chief. "Wow," whispered the youngster in awe, "look at the sheriff!" The Stevenses are adding a Fresh Air this year to their own four children. We kind of think—city kids feeling as they do about "cops"—that the Stevenses' little visitor will be the best-behaved child in town. Until he finds out that a cop, like anybody else, can be a small boy's friend.

Richard and Jackie Gilpatrick of Springvale saw Fresh Airs in their friends' homes and decided this year they'd have them too. They have no children of their own but he teaches industrial arts in junior high school and she teaches first grade, so both are on to the ways of the young. They're going to try to show their visitors things they might not have seen before, a game preserve for one, and of course there'll be fishing on Mousam Lake from the Gilpatrick's boat.

Mrs. Clayton Freeman of Saco (she's John Downing's half-sister, by the way; taking Fresh Airs seems to run in families this year) has two children of her own, a boy and a girl, and is taking one. When her pharmacist husband starts his vacation July 31, they're taking off for camp at Little Sebago. One of her two children is going to be disappointed at first. Each wants a child of his own sex as a Fresh Air playmate.

Cape Neddick was represented by Mrs. Haven Freeman whose husband works at Portsmouth Naval Shipyard. They had a Fresh Air once through the Dover Committee and tried to get him back but he had moved away. This year she decided to try through Kennebunk. There'll be beaching and picnics for her little guest in company with her own six- and four-year-olds.

The Lester Meyerhoffs of Sanford had asked for an eleven-year-old boy. We had just started interviewing them when the bus showed up. (Did you get him, Meyerhoffs?) Their interest in Fresh Airs was sparked by her mother who is a school nurse in Sanford.

Last to descend from the bus, looking fresh as daisies, were the Frederick H. Lewises, Bud and Gini, who escorted the children up from New York, depositing little groups at other Friendly Towns along the way.

Bud Lewis has been at his job as head of the Herald Tribune Fresh Air Fund for twenty years. His wife was an elementary school teacher and now teaches remedial reading at the East Harlem Protestant Parish. The trip held no terrors for them. "It was so well organized," said Gini Lewis. "They thought of everything. Dramamine, upchuck bags, rope for bursting suitcases. Everything!"

Bud once taught psychology at Bates College and Simmons. Then came World War II, from which he emerged a lieutenant commander. At Iwo Jima he had struck up a friendship with Whitelaw Reid. "He was 'Whitey Reid' in the service," says Bud Lewis. "I played chess with him, and we discussed the world situation. I never guessed he was one of the Herald Tribune family."

Back in New York a few years after the war, the casual friendship bore fruit in Bud's being asked to assume leadership of the Herald Tribune Fresh Air Fund. "That summer of '46 we sent four thousand children to Friendly Towns and our camps. Last summer we sent fourteen thousand. Since 1946 we've gone from a budget of one hundred fifty thousand to six hundred fifty thousand dollars.

"Our camp counselors are the very best. They have to be dedicated because we can't pay them as much as private camps do. We have seven camps for underprivileged children: Bliss, Anita, Hayden, Marks Memorial, Pioneer, Coler, and Hidden Valley. This last specializes in crippled children."

The Kennebunk area holds a warm place in Bud Lewis's heart because nearly all its host families ask for Black or Puerto Rican children, a request not often coming from other Friendly Towns. "On the way up," said Gini Lewis, "one of the children told me, 'My house is white.' I asked her if she meant that her house was painted white. She said, 'No, that's not what I mean. The family I'm going to is white.'"

Fund records are full of the stories of successful men and women whose first experience with a decent and healthy way of life they trace to their childhood Friendly Town visit. Unfortunately, there is never enough money to take care of all the children who should have this experience.

Friendly Town's annual country vacation for city kids is still going strong. The operation has a new title, *The Fresh Air Fund*, (the *New York Herald Tribune* having expired but leaving behind this starry memorial to its long existence). The Fund's budget is now six million dollars, every penny spent on giving a constantly growing number of city-trapped children two weeks (longer if hosts wish) of fresh air, swimming and games, and learning about nature and life as it's lived country style. The Fund includes – as well as the Friendly Town operation – owning and operating seven summer camps in Dutchess County, New York. Present chairperson for Maine is Mrs. Gloria McBride, fund representative for the state, who lives in Kennebunk and will answer questions from her home, 9 Fieldcrest Drive, Kennebunk, ME 04043; phone (207) 985-4898. But checks and money orders should be sent to *The Fresh Air Fund*, 1070 Avenue of the Americas, NY, NY 10018.

Two Fire Watchers' Jobs

September 13, 1967

IN A SIX-BY-SIX glass cubicle atop a tower outside Sanford sits a young woman. She climbed the tower at nine this morning and won't come down until six tonight.

Below is a trailer, her home during the summer. A little beyond are a farmhouse, an A.T.&T. microwave tower and a smaller one that beams waves through Channel 6. From her own tower the woman looks over vast carpets of forest to distant towns, and on clear days to the White Mountains.

The cubicle is furnished with a map-covered table, two straight-backed chairs, a small oil stove, and a short-wave radio. To keep her company are magazines and books. Sometimes, a visitor climbs the 73 steps out of curiosity or for the view.

The young woman wears her dark hair short and straight. She has large brown eyes and a come-and-go smile. In slacks and a boy's shirt open at the neck, she looks much younger than her thirty-three years. "It's the good fresh air up here," she says.

For nearly four years Anna J. Woodward of York has been official fire watcher at the Mt. Hope tower. She works seven days a week from the time the snows first leave the ground in April until fall rains or snows start in November. Rainy days are off unless "the boss has something else for me to do," like painting, mowing lawns, cutting and spraying bushes. (In the foggy dew of this summer she's had the most days off from the Tower she's ever had.)

"My ambition was to be a lobsterman," she says ruefully. She did do lobstering for about ten years, but what with "wreckings" (when your gear is lost) it got kind of discouraging.

She grew up loving outdoor life, one reason she has her tower job now. "It's like prison if you have to work inside," she says. She looked around at the room where we sat. "Of course, I'm cooped up here, but I can open the windows and let the fresh air in."

Anna had no special training for her job of fire watching. A ranger climbed the tower in the beginning to explain the rudiments, but she learned mostly from her short-wave and by reading manuals. Her fire watching covers the Kennebunks, Alfred, Lebanon, Acton, Shapleigh, Sanford and Springvale. She starts her day with a weather report that she passes on to anyone who wants it, from Kennebunkport to York, on the Coastal Fire Company's frequency. "Hardly anybody ever calls me about the weather," she says, "but they can. Just dial 207-324-3961."

"At one, I send in a fire danger code to Ogunquit." Daily she bends over a chart to fill in Spread Index (fire danger degree on the Smokey Bear "Class Day"), Temperature, Fine Fuel (pine needles, twigs, etc.), Herbaceous Stage (state of vegetation), Build - Up (how a fire will behave once started), Wind Direction, Wind Ground Speed, and Rain. "All day, of course, I'm watching for fires. If I see active smoke I notify the town warden or fire department of the area and then call the forest ranger. If there's a forest fire I let the rangers know how deep the fires are going to burn into the ground. I have to be on watch for lightning strikes sometimes for a couple weeks after a storm. It takes that long sometimes for a smouldering fire to burst out."

We were examining the chart when our peripheral vision caught a lazy white feather curling above distant trees. We straightened up, excited. "Look," we said, pointing.

Anna plunged us back into amateur status. "That's only the Sanford dump. It's what we call a fixed, or friendly, smoke — like a factory. We don't report those."

Beyond the windows no stir of human life was anywhere. Hardly even a house could be seen except those nearly hidden by trees. But the leaves began to ripple and the wind whined and the tower swayed. Our inner ear at once rebelled. We grabbed hold of the table. Anna laughed. "You ought to be up here some days when the wind gets up to twenty or thirty miles an hour. Then it really sways. And it rattles so you can't hear the radio."

Is it lonely for her here in the cubicle? Does she ever long for human companionship? "Not especially. I get bored sometimes. In between watching for fires and doing my chores I read or listen to the radio or write letters. I talk on the short-wave to other watchers sometimes, or the coast guard. In the fall I watch the deer grazing down there in the clearing." She laughed. "I could shoot them from up here, but I don't think my bosses would approve." After a pause, she said, "Yes, I suppose I'm bored sometimes. But not lonely."

Off season Anna works in a restaurant and goes fishing and hunting. Summers, when she comes down from the tower, she and the woman who shares her trailer relax in lawn chairs and talk over the day. Sometimes they take a ride down the mountain to the coast to visit friends.

But Anna's real life is in the tower. "It's beautiful in the fall," she said, looking down at the green rug of trees that fade into a lavender haze at the horizon. In imagination we saw the scene as it would be in a few months, the trees transformed into an Oriental carpet, deer grazing peacefully below. We smelled the fresh pine air; heard, in between the short-wave's chatter, the silence broken by the rustle of a chipmunk or squirrel scurrying through the underbrush.

The tower was indeed a place to "sleep, perchance to dream . . . " if it weren't for those pesky wisps of smoke.

Anna Woodward was done with forestry last fall. How did she feel about leaving her years of service? She doesn't yearn for it. "When I got down from that tower for good, I felt ten years younger." So who does the watching now? "Firemen volunteer for weekends," Anna told us. "The rest of the time there is no watch." Reason? The state of the Maine State budget.

October 4, 1967

LOW BRANCHES beat a tattoo on our car. We jounced up the narrow mountain road through holes and over jagged rocks. Finally the car sputtered in protest. We turned the key, leaving her to recover while we climbed the rest of Ossipee Mountain on foot.

The mountain dozed in the afternoon heat. A bee's z-m-m-m sounded like a distant plane. A bird called with startling clarity. On either side of the path, trees rose clean from carpets of pine needles or nestled their trunks into ferns and underbush. A smell of blueberries was in the air.

We began to be winded. The mountain, 1,058 feet high and located in Waterboro, is labeled a "hill" on the map. Now it seemed another Everest, lacking only snow and llamas. A sign "Drink to forest fire prevention" led us down a side path to a spring and a tin dipper. The place was mossy and smelled of damp earth. There was a twilight stillness there, and the water from the dipper was cold and pure. That there is a spring not far away, with water clear as melted crystal, bears noting in these days of pollution.

Back on the main path. Past crumbling stone walls (walls on a mountain?), past a clearing, past woods and more woods, until a noise stopped us. It was a sound of something falling in the dense trees, then movement through the undergrowth. We saw nothing. The sound stopped and we climbed on. At the top of the mountain a grove of slim young birches formed a curtain for a clearing. We came out to where rock mounds glinted in the sun and poplar and aspen leaves flashed and chattered. At the edge we looked down on scattered rooftops and the china gleam of Little Ossipee Lake set like a sapphire in forests that stretched as far as the eye could see.

A tower dominated the clearing. We passed a "Welcome" sign, climbed forty steps to a trap door and met the smiling face of Wayne Foss, fire watcher. "What was that noise back there?" we asked, describing the falling sound and the movement through the woods.

"I don't know," he said, then added, "could be bears. Three of them were shot up here a year or so ago." Was he putting us on? We couldn't be sure. Now about those stone walls. A little odd, wasn't it, stone walls on a mountainside? The mountain, he said, was once cleared land. Between 1850 and 1900 it was covered with farms. The last one burned before the 1947 fire.

"There's a stone marker down there," Wayne said, "with 'McLucas Farm, 1848' on it. There used to be a road up the mountain during stage coach days. Someone even built a ship up here. Got it down in winter on sleds pulled by oxen and put it in at Kennebunkport."

Wayne's tower room is larger by far than the ones at Mounts Hope and Agamenticus. It had the usual table with map spread out, the usual radios, mikes, binoculars, and Smokey Bear literature, the usual windows giving out on the usual spectacular view. Something in the room, though, had been missing from the other watchtowers we'd visited—a wooden crib in a corner labeled "Mark J. Foss, 3-27-1967."

"My son," explained Wayne, laughing. "I used to keep him up here sometimes when he was little. Now he crawls around and gets into everything, so he stays down below in the trailer with his mother."

Wayne is twenty-four. He was born in Hollis and went to school in Limerick. Because his father is a trapper and a hunter, he was brought up in the woods and loves them. ("Anything I can do to preserve the woods I'll do.") And he deplores irresponsible shooting in the hunting season. "There's a lot of death. But that's better than half-killing. There should be a law to make hunters use high-calibre rifles instead of buckshot. If you can't kill clean, then miss clean. Don't just half-kill."

Wayne's fire watching covers all of York County, parts of Cumberland County and New Hampshire. He looks out over dwindling evidence of the '47 fire, silvered dead trees that emerge from the new growth like candles from a cake. "Most of it has come back to hardwood," he says, "but there are a lot of small pines. Eventually they may push their way through the hardwood." At the edge of a promontory, a hundred yards or so from the tower, a white flag was whipped by the breeze. "A couple boy scouts camped out there last night. They have their names written on the flag." Wayne has enough visitors—a thousand last season—to break the monotony. "I thought the job would be lonely when I took it, and in a way it is. You have to like it or you wouldn't stay five minutes."

The breeze stiffened into a wind. Below, three boys and a man started to climb the tower. It was time to leave. We wanted reassurance that there would be no bears on the way down, but we didn't want to voice our fear. Wayne just might have been kidding about those bears. We went down the path, ears cocked for unusual sounds, eyes searching the woods. No bears. We saw instead the sharp green of ferns against dark tree trunks, the fragile green umbrellas made by leaves up where the sun warms the tops of trees, pale sunlight that misted the forest like a shining fog.

The car came in sight. We ran. We rolled up the windows against bears, drove down the mountain and out onto the highway. We glanced back at the tower. It looked flimsy at this distance, like a tower built by a child out of matchsticks. "Matchsticks" is a bad word in Maine woods. Smokey Bear says, "Always hold matches till cold. Be sure to drown all fires. Crush all smokes dead out." We would, certainly, and we could feel free of fire threat too because of these three young watchers—Anna Woodward at Mt. Hope, Russell Horning at Mt. Agamenticus, Wayne Foss at Ossipee Mountain—who spend their days in lonely towers watching for smoke.

Rotary To The Rescue

January 31, 1968

LAST WEEKEND Mrs. Arthur Smith of Hartford, Connecticut, was in Kennebunk to attend the wedding of her granddaughter, Cheryl. Saturday night at 8:00 P.M. she suffered a heart attack.

She had a history of such attacks, so her son, Fred Smith of Kennebunk Beach, knew what to do: call a doctor who would give her medication and send her, if necessary, by ambulance to the hospital. In the meantime she must not be moved.

Fred Smith started dialing. The phone rang unanswered at the houses of two of the Kennebunks' seven doctors and osteopaths (later one did answer). Four whom he did reach would not, or could not, make a house call. Somewhere in his phoning Mr. Smith called Webber Hospital. A doctor was on call there, he was told (they could not reveal his name), that Mr. Smith must bring his mother to the hospital. Fred Smith knew from past experience he must not move her without a doctor's orders. He resumed phoning.

Finally the office of Dr. William Bergen, a D.O., answered. Dr. Bergen, Mr. Smith was told, was away for two weeks, but his calls were being taken by another osteopath, Dr. James Henick, newly arrived in town and not yet in the phone book. "He came immediately," Mr. Smith told the *Star*. "He affirmed that my mother was having a heart attack. He said we must get her to the hospital by ambulance. I called Communications in Kennebunk. They got one here very quickly and took her to Tri-County Hospital in Kittery. She's responding to treatment, but she'll be there quite a while."

His was not an isolated case, according to Fred Smith. People he has talked to since have told him of similar experiences during these past several months of acute physician shortage in the Kennebunks. According to the Maine Medical Association (MMA) one doctor per 2000 people is considered adequate. The Kennebunks' four MD's and three DO's for about 5800 population sound like plenty. Two of the doctors, however, for health reasons, have drastically restricted their practice, and one has suspended his, leaving one medical doctor and three osteopaths practicing regularly. There is, moreover, no assurance that the towns ever have at least one doctor at a given moment available in case of emergency. Worried individuals have been making attempts to interest a physician in coming to the Kennebunks, and now the Rotarians have begun action.

"We've already talked to Carleton Davis, administrator of Webber Hospital," says Henry Twombly who with Hiram Clifford comprise the committee named by Rotary the first of this month to look into the problem, "and with Dr. Paul Hill, Jr., head surgeon at Webber and president of the Maine Medical Association. Also we wrote Dr. Daniel Hanley in Brunswick, Executive Secretary of the MMA." (Dr. Hanley is physician for the Olympics. Before leaving for Grenoble he sent a folder of instructions on procedure for securing a new doctor.)

The Kennebunk-K'port Chamber of Commerce, also concerned about the problem, sent out a questionnaire last summer to the seven doctors of the Kennebunks. Compiled by Dave Walley, the survey asked in essence: Does the community need more doctors? There were five replies. No, said four. Yes, said one. One thought the population should reach 8000 before the question of another doctor was considered. Two thought nothing should be done till the figure got to 12,000. And one, not till the 14,000 mark.

"In finding a doctor," Twombly went on, "it is necessary to get someone acceptable to Webber. And we prefer a general practitioner, of course.

We'd like one young and vigorous enough to go out on house calls. Trouble is, young doctors go into research or they specialize."

Dr. Hill, mentioned above, thinks too that the problem is not an easy one. "There are seven hundred doctors practicing in Maine," he said. "This is two hundred more than is considered adequate according to the one doctor for every two thousand population figure, but it is distribution that is bothering. Young men are loath to practice in small towns and especially if hospital facilities aren't near." Out of last year's graduating class at Harvard Medical School, Dr. Hill went on, only one preferred country practice to city.

He favors plans providing for "group doctors" whereby three or more physicians share a suite of offices, a secretary and a nurse(s), thus assuring the continuous availability of at least one doctor "twenty-four hours a day, seven days a week." Better known elsewhere than in Maine, it has been adopted successfully in some communities in this state, notably Ellsworth and Brunswick. Dr. Hill suggests that a nucleus for such a group already exists in the Kennebunks. "The doctors you have," he says, "are experienced and know the particular problems involved."

The difficulties of getting a physician for towns like the Kennebunks, he thinks, are great. Doctors just coming out into practice might apply (and they, as has been said, are mostly interested in specializing) or older men who are fed up with city life. But he and the MMA, he says, will do their utmost to help. He plans to bring the matter up at the MMA's next council meeting.

In the meantime, Messrs. Clifford and Twombly, representing Rotary, are hot on the trail of the elusive new doctor. "Any comments," says Hiram Clifford, "that the townspeople might care to make to help us in our search, we'd be glad to hear."

The doctor famine that earlier plagued southern Maine, and no doubt other villages and towns throughout the country, has pretty much disappeared. It was cities that had always magnetized young medics for whom fame and fortune had been goals, but in the sixties and seventies these young men, even older ones, began moving northward. A good percentage settled in the southern Maine coastal region.

The migration was often caused by the lure of a nearby office ("commuting" having become a dirty nine-letter word); nearby good schools for their children; nearby golf and tennis courts; and the nearby sea. Life for these medics became less stressful and furnished family "togetherness," a popular word at the time.

Clinics appeared. Now there was always a doctor or surgeon at hand, assuring medical help in emergencies. Sirens of ambulances began to be heard, these vans of mercy whisking their occupants to hospitals that gradually became larger and better equipped than those of the "doctor famine" days. The ambulance is usually part of the volunteer fire department's equipment and so serves the double purpose of transporting the sick and wounded and of answering fire alarms.

Voluntary service, in the way it usually operates in small communities ("one-big-family" style), is a relic of the past that is still alive and active. Another is that rare doctor who on occasion will make a house call.

"Please Tell Us First"

July 23, 1969

IN WELLS LIVE three special dogs. They are large, playful, friendly, inclined to slobber a bit. They rate an interview because they are Maine's official bloodhounds.

Once they lived in Vermont, until the State Police there presented them to Maine. The gift put them into the hands of State Trooper Robert Mitchell of Wells.

Trooper Mitchell, now their handler, has learned so much about the breed that he gives a course, four hours of bloodhound history and tracking, at the State Police Academy in Augusta where Maine policemen meet annually to be briefed on new equipment and techniques.

Bloodhounds, Mitchell learned, are mentioned as far back as 727 B.C. and are thought to be the original hunter of dogdom. Monks of the early Christian era used to keep them. Crusaders brought them back to Europe from Constantinople, and Norman conquerors took them across the channel to Britain. They have won their greatest acclaim in the United States for tracking down fugitives and lost persons. "A bloodhound can trace a thief who has stolen a car and abandoned it," says Mitchell. "He can get the scent off the seat, even if the thief sat there just a short time." "Any dog," Mitchell went on, "can distinguish human perspiration, even diluted to one part to a million, but no other breed excels the bloodhound on a cold trail." A trail is considered cold after ten to twelve hours. In 1954 a bloodhound called "Doc Holiday" broke the record, tracking a trail that was fourteen days and one hour cold.

Four types of persons require bloodhound search: wandering mental cases, escapees, thieves, and the lost. The first two give you a problem, says Trooper Mitchell. Usually they do not want to be found, and when found are fearful. They are fearful of the dogs because the public has a concept of bloodhounds based on what they have read (*Uncle Tom's Cabin*, etc.) of them, hell-bent for their quarry, intent on gobbling it up in ravenous snaps of their dripping jaws.

Not so, says Mitchell. "Bloodhounds are among the most docile of dogs. They go slowly along the trail, step by step. And they are very silent. They don't bark. They are just too busy. If it's a lost child they'll run up and lick it, as much as to say, 'Well! Here you are!'"

Trooper Mitchell uses his own children in training the dogs – Bonnie Jean 16, Robert 14, and Polly Ann 13. Wendy 8 and Deborah 6 are too young, but both play with the dogs, and Debbie is tickled that one of them came already named Deborah.

One of the children, taking the part of "runner," begins playing with the young dog and giving him treats of meat, usually the boiled liver they love. After a while of this, the runner goes a short way off and hides. The dog, with his handler, will work his way up to the hunted. Next, the runner leaves his jacket a short way from the dog and hides again until the dog works up to him. The bloodhound is always rewarded by praise and meat.

When the dog has mastered these two initial steps, the runner makes a longer trail, attaching bits of colored paper on trees along the way, so the handler can tell if the dog is following the trail. Finally the dog is given a sniff of the runner's clothing. He sets off on a real hunt and when he finds the hunted, this time he has in effect graduated.

Bloodhounds must start the trail with a piece of clothing belonging to the hunted. It must not have been laundered. It must not even have rested next to clothing worn by other members of the family, as in a laundry basket. Dogs go to their target most successfully after a whiff of underthings, but sometimes a bed sheet or blanket can be used. The piece of clothing should be handled as little as possible. Ideally it is placed in a bag and sealed pending the dogs' arrival.

Damp days are best for trailing, but not too damp; water obliterates the scent. Dogs can track as well in darkness as in daylight, but darkness makes it hard for the handler, so most tracking is done in daytime. The paved streets of urban areas present problems but, says Mitchell, "when Charley Black was shot – he was one of the troopers in that South Berwick bank holdup – the dogs took the scent right through the streets."

Two dogs are taken in a trailer to the start of the search, but only one is used. The other is a spare in case he is needed. Pliers are carried to remove porcupine quills, an occupational hazard. In between official searches the dogs are kept in trim with two or three practice runs a week.

Before our interview with Mitchell ended, there was one thing the trooper wanted to say: "Most important of all, please," he begged, "PLEASE put in something about the family getting in touch with us first when anyone is lost. Usually they panic and start looking themselves, and then everybody else looks, and by the time the dogs get there, the track is obliterated."

In only two instances, he says, may it be important to start out on your own. One is when the person is lost in some remote part of the state, too far away for the dogs to get there quickly ("but call us just the same"). The other is when someone is lost in the dead of winter and might suffer from exposure.

Paul Gallagher, State Trooper, works in New Gloucester, Maine, at a satellite of the Maine Criminal Justice Academy. He is the latest trooper to take the place of Mitchell (see above). Following Mitchell no dogs were used for several years until late in the seventies when it was decided to bring dogs back, to simplify the troopers' work in tracing lost persons, escapees, children, etc.

Rather than bloodhounds now, two German shepherds were obtained and in 1980 two more were added, one having been trained by the Connecticut state police, the other by the Massachusetts state police. This proved so successful that in 1983 a new skill was added to the dogs' education – they would henceforth help in locating narcotics. From that time on the troopers have had at least one patrol dog school – although at this writing that school is on hold owing to budget problems.

Gallagher trains the dogs himself with the aid of an assistant trainer and fourteen teams (men with dogs assigned to them). These dogs are not penned; they live in the men's homes where bonding of the dog with his trooper is intensified. After a month of training and close relationship they are tested and, if proven up to par, are recertified every six months. The partnership of man and dog lasts for from six to eight years of service that covers the area from Kittery to Fort Kent. The dog is then reassigned in retirement to his officer. Cost of each dog per year is $1,000 to $1,700; this includes medical treatment when necessary. A "bomb" dog is assigned to each unit. It checks buildings, cars, etc. One bomb dog got shot and had to be retired to his handler for life.

The dogs put their lives on the line for their troopers. Many have been injured but have been cured physically. If the trauma has not affected their acuity, they are returned to work.

The School Around Us

October 13, 1971

"CHILDREN ARE NOT half an adult. That is one of the most serious misconceptions around. Children are whole beings. People assume that children are clumsy, that they don't have serious goals . . . "

A young man is speaking. He speaks evenly, his expression is gentle. Like many of his age he is longish haired and bearded. His teeth are very white, his dark eyes intelligent. He half sits, half reclines in a chair while he talks, holding a tow-headed infant son in his lap. His other tow-head, scowling with three-year-old intensity, pushes a miniature red truck on the floor.

The young man's wife sits in a nearby chair. Like her husband she is slender and dark haired ("but we both were blond as children"). Dark circles smudge her eyes, and she lets her husband do most of the talking. Both are tired. In this short time since their arrival in Maine, they had moved into a house, met with countless parents and well-wishers, and pitched in with the parents to ready The School Around Us (twenty-four

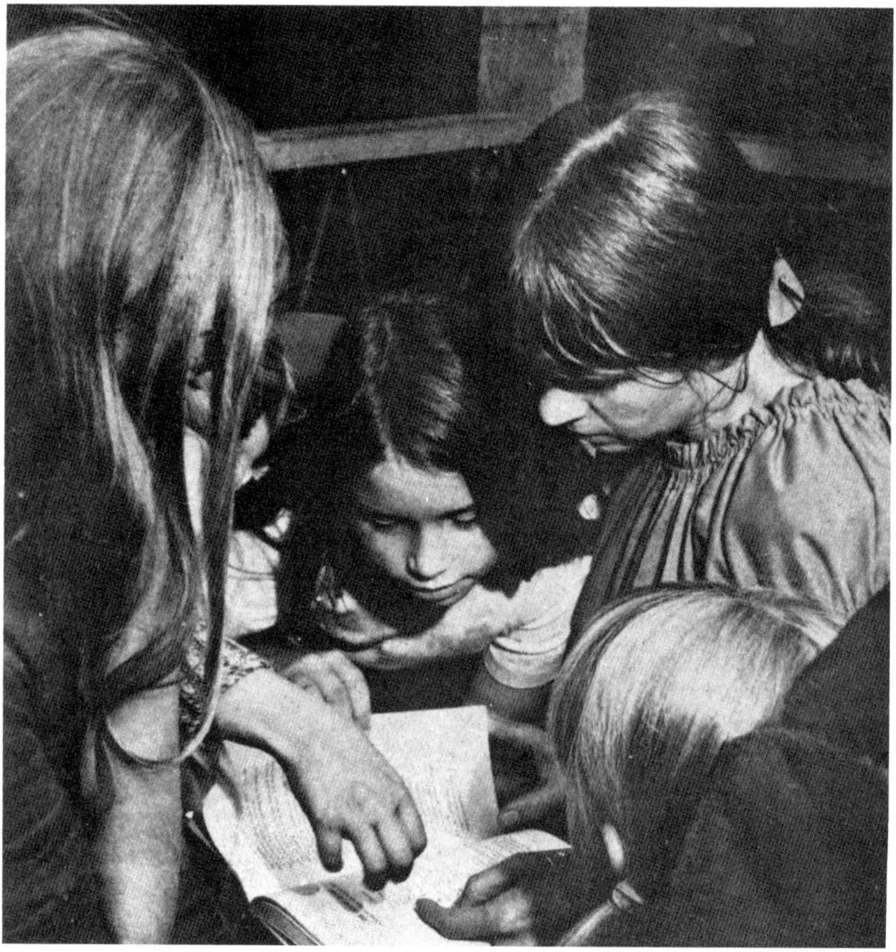

"What does he mean, right here, when he says . . . ?" / Photo by the author, 1972

children registered) for the opening of its second year. At the time of the interview this was due in three days and there was still much to be done.

The young couple, Mark and Merrily Dupree, are new teachers for the School. They come from Colorado where both did their undergraduate work at Colorado State. Both got their MA's from the University of Nebraska, and both are working toward their PhD's. While working on his doctorate Mark has also been a full-time instructor at the University of Nebraska for the past two years, and for the last three has participated in a project designed to bring together people involved in elementary education to learn how to deal with problems they may encounter in open classrooms.

Open classrooms? Mark explains: "That is everything from a classroom that has no desks, giving the child freedom of movement, to the so-called free school that we have here [in the School Around Us]." The free school is conducted with a modicum of direction of the child's activities. It enables him to pursue his education at his own pace, letting him explore whatever has fascination and meaning for him at a particular time, letting him develop without crippling pressures on his natural capacity and instinct for learning. Children, says Mark, are naturally curious and want to learn—when furnished appropriate stimulation and environment.

The Duprees have no preconceived plans or projects for the present teaching year. "The more I would plan," says Mark, "the less it would involve the parents with the children. I have lots of ideas. But unless they come from parents as much as from myself—the more the school is structured, in other words—the more you find you're into all sorts of things you intensely want to have succeed." This intensity, he believes, makes for frustration, and the more frustration the more a tendency to fail.

Aside from its being a school they want their own children to attend, it was the idea of parents involving themselves, emotionally and financially, to the extent they do in The School Around Us that decided the Duprees on choosing it in preference to other free schools where they might have applied as teachers. "Obviously," says Mark, "this school struggles from day to day [there is no fixed tuition; parents pledge to pay what they can]. But we wanted to make a commitment to some place that involved parents so directly. This is a community," he went on, "that actually got itself together enough to make a building. The School was built, brick by brick, by the hands of parents. This is unique. Usually such a school is financed by someone with money or by some foundation."

He stopped. Ivan, his three-year-old, had found a marble on the floor. "Better pick it up," Mark said, "or Colan will swallow it. He'll suck it up like a vacuum cleaner." Mark's mouth formed itself into the hole of a vacuum hose; he made a whirring noise that ended in a sound of suction. Ivan laughed. He handed his father the marble and went back to his truck.

All the work of the School except teaching is done by volunteers, usually the parents. Among these are two carpenters, five teachers, a draftsman, a chef, a lawyer, a doctor—and one man who, for profit, drags logs out of the Saco River to make wide boards. School equipment is either donated or bought, second-hand for the most part.

A man in Saco is donating a much-desired tape recorder. "Once the children start dictating stories, it's amazing what they can do, even four- and five-year olds. A recorder has unlimited use—recording bird sounds, for example." Mark publishes the children's poems and stories on his own small handpress. "The children are tremendously impressed when they see their work in print."

Latest report on the comfortable success of the School Around Us: "We are full," says staff member Claudia Berman. "Full" means thirty-three pupils of prekindergarten age through eighth grade. Enrollment is limited to that number (one teacher to ten pupils) in order to conduct the kind of education SAU feels is important in developing the child's potential. Its brochure states:

We work hard to insure that children retain their natural love for learning. Pupils are encouraged to work at their own level of development. Divergent thinking is encouraged and children learn there is often more than one *right answer . . . And . . . we are all constantly learning from the world in which we live.*

General acceptance of the school's philosophy at first was slow in coming. But now "we are becoming a model for public schools in experiential, student-centered education. The staff," Berman continues, "often holds in-service workshops on hands-on science and integrated education." In addition to the staff of three teachers, four or five interns come at a time from the Universities of New England and Southern Maine to learn, and participate in, SAU's teaching methods.

The school has no director; it is still parent-run cooperatively. Its original mortgage has been paid and a remortgage arranged for necessary renovations to the building. Three annual craft fairs help finance SAU's operation. "These fairs have earned a reputation for carrying some of the best craftwork in the state."

So here is a dream that made it, spewing forth into the world around them smart, socially-conscious, creative, and occasionally "bumptious—but alert" young adults.

A Reformatory Re-Forms

January 26, 1972

LARRY SAMPSON (not his real name) got in trouble with the law and is now in the South Windham Reformatory. Let's see how Larry is "processed."

He is assigned a room. He is given a physical and psychological examination. He goes before a classification board for tests to determine which of the reformatory's trade schools he will work in. (He has never had any job training; his longest employment has been six weeks.) He will have a remedial reading course he sorely needs because of his lack of education and if he qualifies, he will get special tutoring for a high school equivalency certificate.

His regimen at the prison starts. In the Automotive Department Larry begins to learn tune-ups and repairs, front-end alignments and tire balancing and repairs on outboard motors and lawn mowers. Others of his fellow inmates meanwhile are busy with woodworking, electrical work, prefab construction, welding, or graphic arts. Larry will also learn how to make out a job application and how to conduct himself in a job interview. During a break he goes to the gym for a workout. Come summer he'll go into the yard and play some ball. There is occasional entertainment in the form of a weekly movie, and there is a new library.

Larry's teeth have been found to be beyond repair. They will be pulled and he will be fitted for a full denture by the dentist who visits the reformatory once a week. Larry has also been found to be emotionally disturbed, and while his psyche can't be pulled out and a new one inserted, it will be repaired as much as possible by the psychologist and the psychiatrist who visit on a part-time basis. He will also no doubt visit one of the reformatory's two chaplains, Catholic Father Gerard Bolduc or the Reverend Mr. T. Lawrence Gilbert, a Baptist. Besides their spiritual ministrations to the men, Father Bolduc and Mr. Gilbert conduct services in a small chapel in the buildings.

Ages of inmates at Windham range from sixteen to twenty-six. Larry's is an average nineteen. The average stay is six and one-half months, maximum three years. Recidivism (the return of a prisoner for subsequent crimes or offenses) at Windham is 15 percent. National recidivism is 35 percent.

It was 35 percent at South Windham too a couple of years ago. What has caused the phenomenal drop since then? The works program for one thing, according to Superintendent Merton Johnson. The physical and mental health program for another. Add pastoral counseling and worship services. And probably not a small part is due to the fact that the men who administer the programs at Windham care about their charges and their charges know it.

Superintendent Johnson has been connected with the institution for twenty-nine years, fourteen of them as superintendent. He has seen a lot of changes. He would like to see even more. He would like more work programs. "We have one hundred and twenty inmates, one hundred and twenty different sets of needs. We should have a multiple choice of programs available." He would like a better dining room, better cells, a new and larger chapel. To the argument that if a hotel is made of a prison, wrongdoers might clamor to enter, be loath to leave, Johnson answers, "If you were to select the best hotel with the best service in the pleasantest suite, and were locked up at night . . . " He leaves his sentence in midair; his point is made.

The inmate is locked up. According to the South Windham Reformatory credo, that is his punishment. "From there on we program him to rehabilitation. He is kept busy morning to night. Work and recreation for sixteen hours, sleep for eight." And he is steadily geared for his release. Johnson prefers that it be soon. He does not believe in long-term incarceration. "When they stay in an institution too long they lean on it. It becomes a crutch."

So the prisoners are made as ready to rejoin the world as the institution can make them. Then what? Too often he emerges into a world unready to accept him. Superintendent Johnson, Mr. Gilbert, and others of the reformatory's staff are reaching out into the community to try to change this attitude. At a meeting of penologists and interested persons at Thomaston State Prison, Mr. Gilbert heard Dr. Allan Knight Chalmers talk about this. Dr. Chalmers – who had retired to Kennebunkport several years ago – spoke out of his vast experience in prison reform on how to get community involvement.

Mr. Gilbert, who is certified to provide pastoral care and training in the Center for Clergymen and Theological Students, is undertaking to train clergymen to know what goes on in their local institutions, including prisons, and to help them deal with the youth of their communities. Clergymen coming to South Windham for the first of the twelve-week training periods starting this summer will become thoroughly acquainted with the institution's programs "so they will know when they encounter the inmate what he is talking about." They will learn of the legal processes by which a man comes to the reformatory. And they will get some understanding of the dynamics of youth.

It begins to look as if the Larry Sampsons may have a chance in life after all.

The Men's Correctional Center, established in 1919, underwent a series of name changes until 1976 when it was renamed and became coeducational for ages sixteen and up. The average daily population count has grown from 120 males at the time the above story was written to 630.2 today. Of this number 55.2 are female. The count includes transfers from the Maine State Prison and county jails (as prisoners become eligible for participation in the Center's programs) and a limited number of Federal detainees for the U.S. District Court in Portland. The Center has responsibility too for the Central Maine Pre-release Center in Hallowell, Maine.

The Center's programs are Care; Treatment; Custody and Security; Religious and Educational; Substance Abuse Treatment; Social Services (including assisting residents in adjusting to the Center); Education, Recreation, and Housing Areas.

Public libraries may obtain the Center's annual report. Address of the Maine Correctional Center is 17 Mallison Falls Rd., Windham, Maine 04062.

A Life Style Achieved

June 27, 1973

MOST OF US, contemplating a working career, first get a job. We then find a home near our job. A young couple now living in Kennebunk reversed this procedure. They decided where they wanted to live. Then they pursued the area's job possibilities.

Out in Iowa—where the decision was made after Victoria (Vicki) LaBrie got her master's degree at the university in "children's learning disabilities," and Henry (Hank) LaBrie III his doctorate in communication, with emphasis on "the black press" —Vicki was remembering her Pittsburgh beginnings where "we always locked the door when we went out," where there was too much machinery, with its concomitant dehumanizing of people. And Hank was remembering his own Cresskill, New Jersey, which had become an extension of New York City's huddled masses and polluted air. Where could they escape this kind of living and still be near enough work opportunities in their special fields? Answer—New England. Specifically—Maine.

Odd, at a time when it is mostly the elderly who flock to Maine for year-round living, that two young people should decide to start their careers here. Even odder that Hank give his wife precedence in the matter of their respective work. It was important, he thought, that Vicki's shiny new degree be put in operation right away. "She knew she wanted to teach. I wasn't so sure what I wanted to do."

Job opportunities in an academic bulletin out of Augusta triggered a long-distance call from Iowa to Leo Martin, who was then the Kennebunk's acting superintendent of schools. "Such a pleasant phone call," Hank recalls. "Mr. Martin said, 'You'd like it here. It's an attractive community. The people are so nice . . . ' He was humanistic," a quality Hank and Vicki had found lacking in some of their other job-seeking contacts.

The LaBries drove east from Iowa and spent three days in Kennebunk trying to find a place to live. "We stayed at Hannah Twist's while we looked." They adored Mrs. Twist. (Vicki: "She offered to edge all my pillows with crocheted lace.") The LaBries like older people. They feel their experience is valuable. In Iowa their best friends were two still-active farming couples in their middle and late seventies. "We went to movies with them. Had dinner with them. Learned a lot from them." Association with them created an interest in farming and led to the vegetable garden that flourishes in back of the house Vicki and Hank finally rented in Kennebunk.

This is Caroline Wallace's home at The Landing. Here the LaBries live with five cats, Vicki's quilting and needlepoint paraphernalia and Hank's books and papers—and hats. The aphorism "he wears many hats" was never more literally applicable. Hank is rarely seen with his pate uncovered. Not because of baldness—he has a thick thatch—but just because he loves hats so much he collects them the way others might collect stamps or paintings. Would he remove the one he had on while his picture was taken? "Well," he said, "I won't feel natural." (He was allowed to keep it on.)

In his cap and shirtsleeves Hank looks less the intellectual he must be, judging from his educational achievements, than the coach he is for Kennebunkport's Babe Ruth baseball team of thirteen- to fifteen-year-olds. He prefers this age group. Last year he coached eight- to twelve-year-olds in football but "I don't have the necessary patience with the younger ones. Their attention span is too brief. I'd be explaining a move and they'd be watching a seagull."

Vicki prefers the younger ones. "They're reaching a certain stage in their development. If you can get to them at the beginning of their problems you can do more with them." She has been working with SAD 71* children who may have physically induced learning problems, caused sometimes merely by faulty nutrition and relieved by parents' being helped toward a better understanding of their child's nutritional needs. Or emotionally induced problems—fear of failure, too much pressure, upsetting conditions at home, etc. Working with small groups or with the individual child, Vicki remedies these to the degree possible. "Teachers, having to cope with large groups, don't always have the time to individualize the child, to discover how he learns best."

Is it difficult, handling such a monumental task by herself? Not really. For one thing, Leo Martin has instituted a system that as student teachers, working in their school their junior year, they offer considerable aid. And the work is rewarding—exciting, when you see children with learning disabilities begin to have success. "You start with them at a level where they've

*Maine School Administrative District No. 71

experienced some success, where they can function, and you proceed from there. I stress what probably everyone knows — the importance of rewarding or praising a child when he does what he should, and ignoring his negative behavior, which is usually merely attention-getting." Too often it's when a child is good that he is ignored. "It's so simple," Vicki says. "The first few days you meet children they're pretty good. So I immediately zoom in and start praising them. One teacher had great success with a chart on the wall for only the positive things — like 'Johnny didn't fight today.' Or 'Mary did well in her reading.'"

Vicki and Hank were married four years ago, when Hank was halfway through his master's program. That finished, he began his doctoral on "the black press," a theme he chose on learning one existed. "Here I'd gone through all this education and I was totally ignorant of it!" Not only that such a press existed but that its circulation exceeds 4 million; that it numbers 208 newspapers, mostly weekly; that there are 4 black dailies; and that the first black newspaper began in New York City in 1827. "There was [the equivalent of] a black Pulitzer," he claims, "even a black Hearst. But you don't hear about them."

For the past two years he has commuted to Harvard once or twice a week, reporting to Oscar Handlin at the Charles Warren Research Center, under a postdoctoral research fellowship in American Studies granted him by the National Endowment for the Humanities in Washington. For one so young (twenty-six) he has written copiously, appearing in popular publications like *Parade* as well as in academic quarterlies. The grant that enables him to do his writing — most of his work is done at home — ends this summer.

Will the LaBries then leave Kennebunk? No. Hank has four local options for work in his field; at least one probably will materialize. And an assistant has been hired to help Vicki in her expanding work in the SAD 71 school system. Of course they'll stay.

Besides, what would they do with their vegetable garden? And those five cats?

When you have dependents, you're better off staying put.

Vicki's and Hank's aim was to seek work that would allow them a clean atmosphere, far from cities' pollution, noise, distraction. They would eventually want a farm that they both would work and at the same time carry on the careers for which they had been uniquely trained. Hank would till the soil of the farm, plant vegetable seeds, build an orchard in his spare time. Vicki would fill jars with the harvest, work on the quilting and needlepoint she so loved doing. It was a heavenly dream—and, unlike most such dreams, conceived before reality sets in, it came true for Vicki and Hank.

Vicki became principal of Kennebunk's Park Street Elementary School. Her innovative "praise or ignore" method quickly bore fruit in the pupils' ability to learn faster and better. Also decreased misbehavior was a bonus. Another addition by Vicki to the school's program: the searching out of children needing help in overcoming emotional problems and in working constructively with their peers; these pupils receive special attention. Park Street became the first, and only, elementary school in Maine to be given the national *School of Excellence* award, presented in Washington, D.C. It was one of only two hundred in the country to receive this recognition.

Hank, deciding on at least a portion of his career, taught at Thornton Academy in Biddeford four years, at Boston University seven. These years were interspersed with the founding and conducting of a publishing company. Then, both being lovers of the soil, the LaBries bought a farm in Kennebunkport where they have lived since, joined ten years ago by Henry IV, quickly nicknamed "Ivy," of course. Hank's major farmwork now is hay. "He makes thirty thousand bales a year," reports Vicki, "produces the largest amount to come out of southern Maine. He also *buys* hay during the year and stores and delivers it. It's a real business."

They are happy with the life they chose and worked hard for, immensely pleased it turned out almost exactly as they had planned.

5

Restoring The Past

Volunteer motorman Peter Paras of Scarborough smiles a welcome from Car No. 2710 now in storage at the Trolley Musuem / Photo by Nancy Ames, 1991

Car Number 2710

July 8, 1965

Eine zehnpfennige Fahrt fur ein
funfpfenninges Fahrgeld
Schlangerln in der Gegenwart des
Passagiers durch.

(Translation)
A ten-cent ride for a five-cent fare
Punch in the presence of the passenjare.

Mark Twain

TROLLEY CAR NO. 2710, in a bright red new coat, and looking none the worse for her 3,000-mile voyage as deck cargo from Hamburg, swung into the Trolley Museum yard at the Port aboard a trailer at 11:45 A.M. on Monday. She was immediately interviewed by a reporter from the *Star* through Mr. O. R. Cummings, Superintendent of Passenger Operations at the Museum.

The trolley has been in a whirl, he said, ever since being swung over the side of the U.S. liner *Pioneer Glen* at dockside in East Boston on June 9th. Right away she had to appear at her formal presentation ceremony at the Sheraton Plaza where the German Consul made a speech and members of the Federation of German Agricultural Exporters, who sponsored the gift of the car to the museum, participated. Then there was a parade in South Boston she took part in, and another celebrating Haverhill's 325th anniversary. The Haverhill Barbershop Quartet rode in her during the parade and sang out her windows. Car No. 2710 wound up her Boston stay with several appearances at supermarkets.

She has earned her retirement to the Trolley Museum. She is forty-four years old and has worked hard all her life. Little did she think, while busily conveying passengers in Hamburg that she would be singled out for a restful old age in Maine instead of—horrible thought—being stripped and sold for junk.

It all happened the way it did because a young exchange student from Germany spent a week at the museum bunkhouse in the Port with other trolley buffs. Back home in Hamburg he called on the Transport Company. "How about one of our old trolleys," he said, "ending up in the U.S.A., in Maine, in Kennebunkport, at the Trolley Museum?"

Car No. 2710 is the only German in the Museum group, which is taking on a cosmopolitan flavor with its foreign trolleys, one each from Italy, Japan, Australia, England, New Zealand and Canada – as well as eighty from far-flung parts of our own United States.

Mr. Cummings, who is a volunteer motorman at the Museum, invited us to come along on his scheduled fifteen-minute run. "It will cool you off," he said.

We climbed up onto a fifteen-bench open car of American make, each bench with a seating capacity of five, and learned that collecting two hundred fares a trip was routine for this trolley during the period 1906-1947 when it carried football crowds between the railroad station in New Haven and the Yale Bowl. "People sat on top of each other," said Mr. Cummings. "They hung from anything they could grab hold of and even sat on the roof."

He slowed down for Meserve's Crossing and clanged the bell vigorously. On either side of us were bushes and more bushes, and in the distance only trees. Yet we were in the middle of an imaginary Times Square, traffic threatening us on all sides.

We got through. "Look at the ads," directed Mr. Cummings. We looked up. Bing Crosby, a young Bing with all his hair, offered a carton of Chesterfields. Joe Palooka's cowlick was welcoming immigrants to the U.S.A. We were urged to Buy a Liberty Bond. We'd be as pretty as the bride smiling down at us from beside a cake of Welcome Soap, if we'd use it. U.S.A. soldiers scowled and held up OUR FLAGS, beseeching us to BEAT GERMANY.

We rolled along the tracks. It was pleasant. The sun was warm, the breeze cooled our face and we smelled blueberries. Blueberries? In June? It was only the memory of bumping over trolley tracks from Portland to Old Orchard in our childhood in a trolley car like this one, inhaling the fragrance of sun-hot berries on those long-ago August days.

"The track we're on," Mr. Cummings was saying, "is part of the original trolley line in existence from 1907 to 1927. We have an agreement with the power company that will permit us to extend our tracks. Next year we'll double our present run. And we're starting work on another car barn. We'll have three barns in the next four years."

The car came to the end of its run at Syracuse. Mr. Cummings rolled the sign above him to Arundel. We turned our seat so we faced in the opposite direction, and a young man in impeccable motorman's outfit started to ride us back while Mr. Cummings talked.

"Most of the work of the museum is done by volunteers," he said. "They take a few days off, or their vacations, to come and run it. We have a Methodist minister here now from Camden, New Jersey. He's spending three days here, just to run the cars."

"Arundel! Last stop!" called the motorman from the front. The trolley slowed to a halt. We jumped down and walked over to Car No. 2710. A group of men still stood around her, silently, worshipfully. Some wore motormen's outfits, one wore the striped twill, visor, and kerchief of a repairman. We heard him whisper softly, "She'll be in operation before nightfall."

It was a romantic thing to say, and we thought we saw the glint of a smile on the front window of Car No. 2710.

The museum, founded in 1939, was incorporated in 1941 as The New England Electric Railway Historical Society, Inc. It is popularly known as the Seashore Trolley Museum. "Popular" is the key word here. In the vast choices of entertainment available to Maine's burgeoning tourists, the Trolley Museum ranks among the highest with over forty thousand visitors in 1991.

The museum started with one trolley car, No. 31, bought for $150 from the Biddeford and Saco Street Railroad Company in 1939. No. 31 thus became the granddaddy of the present 230 cars (including subway and work cars). The vehicles come from throughout the USA as well as abroad, for retirement in Kennebunkport on land that has had to expand to accommodate the influx.

The museum is as proud of its cars as are owners of champion race horses; indeed they are as carefully tended. They are fed (electricity), groomed (polished), and placed gleaming on tracks to carry their riders through woodlands to the next town and back. All the vehicles are ride-able, even the oldest, a horse car built in 1893, and an 1895 Budapest sub-way car. The most modern additions are two cars spawned by the U.S. government in 1972 and turned over to the museum like horses put out to pasture when their working days are ended.

"We are the oldest railway-related preservation museum in the world," one of the members told us. "In this country alone there are thirty-two other trolley museums. In the world, a hundred—and it all started here in Kennebunkport!"

York Village

August 17, 1966

YORK VILLAGE is the culmination of a series of events that started in 1605 when an English explorer sailed along the southern Maine coast and captured five Indian braves.

Back in England the braves were exhibited as savages, but Sir Fernando Gorges, a visionary, took three of them into his home and taught them rudimentary English. The tales they had to tell fired his enthusiasm and he determined to engineer a settlement in the new land.

This project became his life work. In the next forty years small settlements grew up along the southern coast. He obtained a charter from the king to create a "Province of Maine" and, jubilant, he ordered a governor's palace to be built for him.

He never occupied it. The war between the Cavaliers and Puritans put an end to his dreams and his health. He was imprisoned for a year, freed, and died shortly without ever having seen the new land or the settlements he had helped create.

But before that, the Indian settlement of Agamenticus had been renamed Gorgeane after Sir Fernando Gorges and was to become the capital of Maine. Only when Massachusetts later gained control of Maine was the name changed to York and with the change came a Puritan suppression of the fun-loving spirit of its inhabitants. Soon their Maypole dances, their games, and love of good food and drink disappeared.

One morning, on February 2, 1692, a young man of the village making the rounds of his traps discovered a pile of Indian snowshoes propped against a boulder. The next instant war-whooping Indians swarmed down on the village, killing or taking captive 150 inhabitants and burning the entire village with the exception of the garrison house, the meeting house, and the old gaol.

The old gaol, (jail), built about 1653, is the oldest continuously used building in America, in succession a jail, school, private dwelling, and now a museum. Stocks once stood outside, their human captives the butt for ridicule and torment, and a whipping post stood ready for those accused of crime who were to receive lashes as punishment. The stocks and post are gone but the building itself is almost unchanged from the days when prisoners were chained to its walls, food was passed into them through a small aperture, and many men (women too) walked from it to the gallows, standing where the Marshall House now stands, to take their last look at the sea before the rope was placed about their necks.

It was the novelist William Dean Howells who saved the old gaol from ruin. Time, rodents, and tramps had all done their damage, but Howells passing by it one day said, "It is worth saving." And that is why you can see it today in York Village, a gruesome reminder of our earliest beginnings in America.

Willowbrook

June 23, 1971

ONE DAY— in Saboomac, a remote lake in the northern Maine woods, a man came close to drowning. Out of his near death has come a nineteenth century village restoration in Newfield.

How? Well, what sense was there, he decided, in someone over age fifty hunting and fishing far from the help that might be needed in an emergency. So Donald F. King, Sr., sought through lower Maine for a spot where a cry for help might reach more than just birds and deer and fish. He found it. He might have called it "Serendipity" instead of "Willowbrook" because when his hunting lodge was finished he looked around and discovered he was in the middle of an almost intact nineteenth century village: general store, stables, tavern, country doctor's home, old mill. It cried out for restoration — tasteful, nostalgic restoration. There would be nothing honky-tonk about Willowbrook.

One of the first things King did, after buying the property house by house, was to have those buildings that needed it swept clean of chicken refuse. "They went through an era when everybody raised chickens," he says. "The ballroom in the Big House was a chicken coop. The upstairs in Dr. Trafton's stable was a chicken coop . . . " King's main problem was the repair of timbers that had been rotted by chicken leavings and by neglect. "I bought Dr. Trafton's house for five thousand dollars and spent forty-eight thousand dollars bringing it back."

King did not want to be mentioned in a story about Willowbrook — (but how can you talk about a baby without once in a while mentioning who gave it birth?) — because all restoration work has been directed by two women from the adjacent town of Limerick, the now Director Mrs. Georgia Perry and her colleague Mrs. Cecile Lepage. They say they had never done such work before, that Donald King taught them everything. What did they know about restoring sleighs? Old timbers? Upholstering furniture? "But Mr. King said, 'You can do it.' So we did."

In one of his trips to Newfield — from Topsfield, Massachusetts, where he is a business executive — King, in khaki pants and workshirt, pipe in hand, wanders about the village. He pauses to talk with his director, with groundskeepers and carpenter and with a visitor, envisioning the while the barbershop, the law office, the mortuary, all to be built in a five-year plan as exact replicas of those of the past and to be added to Willowbrook. "One thing," he says, "I've created employment. And the money has all been spent locally." Beyond a nominal admission charge, no donations either of money or items are accepted at Newfield. King's independence is of the "Maine cuss" variety. "I've dug up everything myself and paid for them. And I've trained young people to run Willowbrook so there'll be continuity."

The project of Willowbrook was not undertaken for profit. "It is my contribution to posterity," King says, and continues, "The nineteenth century has been so neglected. It was a time of industrial revolution. I have great appreciation for anyone who works with his hands, and this was the last great era for that. I thought our younger people should see what actually had been done during that period. It's closer to them than the seventeenth or eighteenth centuries. Our own grandfathers had a sleigh in their barns."

The youngsters can see the sleighs and carriages; in the 1800s Newfield was the largest manufacturer of them in Maine. The youngsters can also see tools-of-trade of twenty-one blacksmiths and forty-two shoemakers who lived in the old Newfield area. And they can see a few thousand other things of the kinds their great-grandparents knew and used.

As for oldsters — perhaps a Willowbrook soothes our spirit. Perhaps it helps us cope with our century, will ease us into the twenty-first, by letting us know we can return — like the inhabitants of Brigadoon — to at least the trappings of our past.

Willowbrook is a nonprofit organization, listed in the National Register of Historical Places. It has expanded considerably since the above was written but still maintains its nineteenth century, small-village aura. Admission is $6.50 for adults, $3.25 for students age six to eighteen, free for children under six. The restoration is open daily from May 15 to September 30. Tour groups, however, may visit at special-group rates during the October foliage season.

An interesting and tasteful brochure is available by mail. Write (Willowbrook, Newfield, Maine 04056) or phone (207-793-2784) Pam King or Georgia Perry (Willowbrook's two managers) for the brochure or added information. The brochure furnishes peeks at various relics of our past century's living. Here are a few:

"*The Ox Sling* . . . a necessary fixture in every small town in New England, where . . . the ox was suspended to be shod. An ox cannot stand on three feet nor did it like to be shod, thus the need for the sling."

Or "*The Unmarried Maiden's Room* over the ice cream parlor. Here lived the lady who had her own private entrance and facilities for all the comforts for her later years."

Or " . . . you will see many of the small things that brought both joy and sorrow to the people of the nineteenth century . . . stencils which bore out the large orchard activities of the times — military paraphernalia which brought much sorrow — scales which kept all men honest — magic lantern viewers which made great home entertainment — ballot boxes which elected their peers and blackball boxes which allowed secret discrimination."

As you wander in and out of Willowbrook's old houses, its school and mill, its firehouse and shops — your transport back into the nineteenth century is made with little feeling of displacement.

The Brick Store Museum

July 16, 1972

Museums:
Buildings that house paintings
or objects once belonging to the
dead . . . don't-touch guards
. . . musty, drafty caverns.

THE IMAGE is changing. Museums now grow more gutsy than fusty. We would hardly recognize, for example, the old Metropolitan, the old Frick, the old Whitney or, for that matter, the old Museum of Modern Art.

The museum of today, besides making available for study and enjoyment its records, its treasures, now:

Arranges its exhibits more attractively and in changing formats. Encourages traveling exhibitions. Displays painting, sculpture, and craftwork of community art groups. Opens its doors to entertainers, to speakers on myriad (not only historical) subjects. Works closely with schools. Sponsors varied and viable programs. And undertakes a host of other activities from which the museum of the past was prone to draw aside its dusty skirts.

Fitting the new concept is Kennebunk's Brick Store. Its walls are expanding (inventively, not architecturally) to the bursting point under the aegis of a forward-looking president and board—who intend, though, that the museum will retain its simple country-store identity, keeping as a main attribute its unique collection of objects in local use during the eighteenth and nineteenth centuries.

The museum anyway has routinely held lectures and previews during the summer; it now plans, on a year-round basis, to multiply them and widen the scope of their appeal. The trustees, believing the museum

Still more Brick than Frick, the Museum's new image as planned in 1972 intended to retain its country store identity / Photo by the author, 1972

should be the focus for the community's cultural activities, propose to schedule public programs in the performing arts, music, drama, and film. Jim Saunders and his board envision little theatre in one of the buildings of the Museum-owned "Barry Block" to fill a long-felt need of the Museum and to make an auditorium available for other community-sponsored programs.

To relate more closely to the schools, the Brick Store held open house last month to familiarize administrators and teachers with the museum and with materials that might be helpful in classroom work. Nearly half the teachers of Maine School Administrative District No. 71—and the superintendent, assistant superintendent, and one of the principals—attended. Six directors answered such questions as: "When was the Brick Store built?" (In 1825 by twenty-six-year-old merchant William Lord.) "When did it open?" (Lord and his partner Henry Kingsbury opened it October 1, 1825.) "Why is it called the Brick Store Museum?" (From the bricks of its facing, fired at a kiln on the Portland Road.) "When did it become a museum?" (In 1936 a small museum and a gallery were started on the second floor; the organization was incorporated in 1940.)

Planning for and perpetuation of the Brick Store as a museum was a consuming interest of Edith Barry, a direct descendant of owner William Lord. Mrs. Edward Bodman is continuing her late sister's interest, but if the museum is to increase its activities it must also increase its membership. Therefore, a drive for support is about to start.

To launch it the museum offers the first hundred applicants for family membership a gift of *Ancient History of Kennebunk*, a book that is a copy of one written in longhand in 1831 by Edward E. Bourne. Each chapter is a "lesson" given the young people of the Sunday school class he taught at what is now the Unitarian Church. The book opens with a facsimile page of Bourne's original manuscript: "History of the town of Kennebunk from its first settlement to the year 1785."

The first settlers of this town have passed away . . . . The scenes of which they were witnesses, the interesting events of their days, the part which they performed on the stage of life, the sufferings, trials and afflictions which they were called [upon] to endure, and in fact, almost everything connected with their history, have also passed away. . . . So that we may almost say with the Preacher, "there is no remembrance of former things . . . "

But standing today in the Brick Store Museum, surrounded by the tools of life of those people, their candles and carriages, their awls, the hammers and tongs of their blacksmiths, their ship-building implements, their saddles and gowns and quilts, the ancient charts and deeds—

Surrounded by these, there is a kind of "remembrance."

The Brick Store Museum is pretty much as it was when the above story was written. Thus its board of directors and staff have protected the integrity of the old store-turned museum. However, an ongoing change is in program expansion—to more rotating exhibits, more lectures, more of the performing arts, more tours beyond the town for the architecturally and artistically inclined, and so on. One addition to the museum's attractions, planned for but not yet realized, was to be a little theater in one of the adjoining buildings that comprise the Barry Block. This may yet come to pass. The Brick Store Museum has a way of making its dreams come true.

Appledore Island

June 20, 1973

APPLEDORE—the forgotten island. It was once a famous summer resort, this southernmost point of Maine, with a broad-verandahed hotel, tennis courts, swimming pool, cottages, and with Celia Thaxter, a literary luminary who held a salon for great personages of the nineteenth century.

Then began the island's wane. Resort hotels rising on the mainland siphoned off guests from Appledore. Celia died. The hotel burned. Cottages, seeing less and less of their owners, fell victim to vandals, strong winter gales, gulls and rats—until at night the beams of nearby White Island light picked up only dead windows, and bushes stirred by the scuttling of rodents. Merely a memory of human life walked—the ghost of an early inhabitant who died in 1671.

Now Philip Babb's ghost is uneasy. His walks are disturbed by the sound of hammers and machinery, of human voices and motorcraft. Appledore is "biologically rich," says Dr. John Kingsbury, Cornell professor of marine sciences and director of the Shoals Marine Laboratory now established on Appledore. "The waters have one hundred twenty-five species of algae, one hundred fifty species of invertebrates," and who knows how many species of fish? "Maybe a hundred."

Dr. Kingsbury, who with his co-workers labors to make the island again habitable, conducts his visitor over an island that is by far the largest of the nine comprising the Isles of Shoals, but Appledore overrun by weeds and bushes is the most verdant. The island's relatively unpolluted waters, the still-firm foundations and beams of its abandoned cottages, and its proximity to active Star Island (Star Island Corporation leases the major part of Appledore to Cornell) influenced its choice for the marine school and laboratory that have been functioning on the island itself for two years.

The school — last summer was its eighth session, the first five were held on Star Island — exposes the undergraduate to marine sciences, helps him choose a specialty and a graduate school and gives him insight on how his work efforts can mesh productively with others. He does his field work on the island and he hears experts, be they commercial fishermen or specialists from universities or the National Marine Fisheries Service. His dinner table bears "most of the commercial (and some not yet exploited) species of fish, shellfish and seaweeds obtainable from the Gulf of Maine . . . "

The school started out with only an abandoned Coast Guard station for habitation and classes. It is becoming increasingly less Spartan. Dr. Kingsbury and company, together with York contractor Dominic Gratta, are building anew or restoring those of the cottages not still individually owned, and converting the cement watchtower left behind when the Navy pulled out.

The tower wasn't all the Navy left behind. Kingsbury, et. al., have made good use ("We're great scroungers") of pipes and tanks and sundry other items deemed useless and left to rust by their former owners. Good use has been found too for steel beams rescued from razed Marshall House in York, and metal waste functions as road fill. Shoals Marine Laboratory is financed mainly by donations; and when something special is needed — like the project's new backhoe — Dr. Kingsbury goes hat in hand to Cornell's alumni for it.

The backhoe and all other automotive equipment winter in a garage which is part of a new utility building, "Kiggins Commons Building," that also houses a repair workshop, the power generator, a fresh-water distribution center, a research lab and a winterized apartment. Kiggins is the sole built-from-scratch structure to date of the Shoals Marine Laboratory complex. One of the old cottages is being converted into a dormitory "with lots of outside doors and the fewest fire hazards possible." No adequate fire-fighting equipment is handy and fire is a great fear of all Shoals islands. Another ancient house will become a teaching lab and library. A new lab building is in the works for this year.

The Shoals Marine Laboratory program is operated chiefly by Cornell but with the cooperation of, and partial funding by, the University of New Hampshire and the State University of New York. U.N.H., for example, uses the island's near-shore environment for a waste disposal experiment designed to test food decomposition as it affects the immediately surrounding water. It aims thus to discover new means of food-waste disposal for communities and industries.

Kingsbury sometimes indulges a scientific curiosity triggered by Appledore phenomena. Someone from Cornell, he thinks, should study the island's rat population which "fluctuates in a remarkable way. There are practically none in the spring but when the gulls start dying the rats start multiplying. And when the gulls disappear the rat population declines. Do they die of starvation? What becomes of them?" He looks at the gulls soaring above him. "How much energy," he asks rhetorically, "is coming onto the island in the form of gulls feeding themselves and their young? What does this mass of marine energy do to the island as it's recycled through the environment?"

Then he turns back to roads needing construction, to the ubiquitous ivy that must be eradicated, to the thousands of problems attendant on the building of an academic village. A helicopter – its whir cutting into the gulls' screechings – passes overhead and hovers above adjacent White Island. Dr. Kingsbury explains that it lands material for the repair of damage wrought on the Coast Guard island by last winter's storms.

"We bring all our stuff over by boat," he says with a touch of wistfulness. "And it's such slow going."

According to the Department of Marine Sciences at Cornell University, Dr. John Kingsbury, "is not around much anymore," having reached professor-emeritus stage. When we interviewed Dr. Kingsbury on the island in 1973 he seemed all a man immersed in his field of work should be — serious, hardworking, and able to inspire those working with and under him.

His dedication apparently paid off: The Shoals Marine Laboratory on Appledore is now the largest undergraduate educational field station in North America, based, our Cornell informant tells us, "on the number of different courses offered annually or the number of enrollments registered — either way."

Maine Canals

date unknown

THE THOUSANDS of miles of canals that vein England's landscape were not duplicated in the New World to any marked degree. America was too busy settling to think about extending commerce much farther than that required by local needs. What did go beyond the settlements was carried along old Indian trails or by boat. These conditions called out for canals that would connect bodies of water edged by settlements.

When canals did make their appearance well into the nineteenth century, in Maine at least, it was to supply demand for products furnished best by the Northeast, namely lumber and dried and pickled fish. To meet the demand the narrow waterway, traversed by long, thin boats, was brought upon the scene. Although slow, it improved on the former method of transport.

Perhaps a baker's dozen canals were built in Maine. The Cumberland-Oxford, named for the counties it serviced, probably most resembled its English prototype.

Hand-dug by Irish immigrants in 1830 (and used until 1870), the C&O Canal bore its narrow boat by towpath horse to Sebago Lake, where sails took it twelve miles up the Sebago to the Songo. There, the crew poled the boat four miles through Songo's winding waters, then two miles through Brandy Pond to Naples, finishing — again under sail — with twelve miles up Long Lake to Harrison.

Activities burgeoned along the C&O Canal. Industries were born, communities grew up around them and the towpaths bristled with inns and facilities for crew, passenger and horse. As described by Hayden Anderson in *Canals and Inland Waterways of Maine*, "All gates (for the locks) were operated by hand by the crews, passengers, or willing bystanders who would push on the balance beams, the water first being released by butterfly valves or paddle gates."

George Washington's report after the Revolution contained for the first time plans for public improvements for the country. The building of canals was recommended. Of the thirty canal companies that had been incorporated in the original thirteen colonies by 1793, three were in the District of Maine. These were the New Meadow's, 1791-1843; Mousam River's, 1792-1846; and the Georges River and Knox canals, 1793-1860. [Only the Mousam's will be mentioned here.]

The Mousam is twenty-two miles long. When discovered by white men, its mouth, southwest of what later became Great Hill, was near a future ferry and wading place on the King's Highway. It flowed to within half a mile of the ocean, turned abruptly to meander west and south for about a mile, and finally bent to meet the sea.

A sandbar at the mouth prevented entrance of large vessels, but small craft had no trouble bringing in machinery in 1762 for Sayward's lumber mill (located probably near the foot of what is now Sayward Street in Kennebunk).

In the early 1790s a petition signed by citizens of Mousam Village (now Kennebunk) resulted in an act of incorporation. The Mousam, the act stated, was not navigable for vessels of more than ten tons, but the landing place at head of tide was conveniently located for commerce with the back country, and there would be advantages to making the river larger. However, it would be necessary to change the course of the river by damming it and digging a channel to the sea.

So the project was begun in 1793, when Nathaniel Spinney contracted to erect the dam and open the new channel to the west of Great Hill.

This also began a series of disasters that finally killed the dream of a canal deep enough to accommodate 300- to 400-ton vessels. Light craft, however, continued to ply the river.

Spinney dug the canal nearly to low water, and got the dam built just in time for a severe storm to carry it off, leaving the Mousam to continue its normal course undeterred. This, together with the death during construction of his brother-in-law, soured Spinney. He withdrew from the project.

Richard Gilpatrick followed with a plan for a new channel. It would be less than a mile long, this time to the east of Great Hill. Trouble plagued this construction too. Nearing the shore, the diggers encountered a massive ledge. Since funds were inadequate for removing it, the canal was opened to the sea with a depth of only seven to eight feet at highest tide. Optimism had been so high during construction that Joseph and Clement Storer placed an order with a shipyard upstream for a 300-ton schooner. The brothers ultimately saw their schooner maneuvered over the ledge with utmost difficulty and the hull severely damaged.

This closed the door on any future sizable vessels for the Mousam. The project was left in an unfinished state for fifty years.

A feasibility study for improving navigation of the Mousam was reopened in 1826, and in March the legislature named Daniel Sewall one of a group of proprietors of the Mousam Canal. Later in the legislative session, a bill to permit lotteries for several projects including the Mousam's was indefinitely postponed. This lost one means of financing the project and dampened the villagers' enthusiasm.

Public outcry began. *The Kennebunk Gazette* carried editorials and letters against the project. Stockholders of the unsuccessful 1792 venture were against it. A proposed factory that was to make the new canal profitable dragged its heels. The 1826 plan never came to fruition.

In 1830 Congress appropriated $200 for a survey to see if the Mousam could be adapted to deep-water navigation. President Jackson (he of our $20 bills) was opposed to federal financing of such improvements and pocket-vetoed the bill.

Still another effort was started in 1846. A petition, unanimously approved at annual town meeting, resulted in a charter act that repealed the 1826 act and formed the Mousam Navigation Company which named Daniel Remich general agent for more canal digging. A strip of land about 1,782 feet was divided into 27 stations and contracts were let for excavating to a depth of 6 feet, width 18 feet.

No ledges or other obstructions were discovered and construction eventually was completed in the fall of 1851. A final contract was let for breaching the sea wall. The canal would end at the sea.

Then something unforeseen arose. It had been assumed, in digging, that sand would be reached at about six feet and that the tides' action would wash the sand out to sea, thus deepening the canal. What came into view at six feet was not sand but layers of "exceedingly tough" turf, as much as two feet thick and impervious to the action of running water.

Further excavation was indicated. But stockholders and villagers were impatient to see the canal in operation. It was decided to open without further digging.

On a day in November of 1851, volunteers cleared rocks from the seawall and beach, and at 11:00 A. M., Mousam water started flowing through yet another channel to the sea.

It was soon clear that the new channel would never be deepened by any action of the tides and that river traffic would continue to be made up only of small craft. All efforts to make a saltwater port of Mousam Landing had failed.

The canals of Maine had their brief day in history. All that remains of them now are names, such as "Canal Street"(s) found in some towns bordering old canals, or the Cumberland & Oxford Canal School in Westbrook.

They live on too in bits and pieces of wood and metal, an anchor or two, some sail blocks, a boat horn – artifacts that for the most part are in private collections or museums. The most notable reminder of canal heydays is the Canal Bank, chartered in 1825 to help finance the C&O.

The C.&O. Canal Association, which could not be located, was formed in 1973 by canal buffs, is dedicated to preserving the canal's memory. An annual meeting is held each winter. Weather permitting, field trips and outings along the canal route are conducted. Some day the association hopes to see restoration of part of the waterway to its original condition "for the enlightenment of those to whom a canal is. . . . heard of but unseen."

The key word here is "part" – portions of the original canal now lie under the Maine Turnpike.

The above story was an insert (especially for the Maine reader) in the *Star*'s publication about a trip made by the author on the Oxford and Grand Union canals in England in 1976.

6

Ghosts

Does the ghost of Charles Swett still wander here today? / Photo by Nancy Ames, 1991

The Abial Kelley House

October 18, 1962

The ghost of forgotten actions
Came floating before my sight;
And things that I thought were dead things
Were alive with a terrible might.

Charles William Stubbs

ON SUNDAY, September 23, 1866, around nine o'clock in the morning, Dr. Charles M. Swett of Kennebunk went into the stable in back of his house, dug his bottle of whisky from the hay where it was his custom to hide it, and took a healthy swig. At noon he was dead of morphine poisoning. It could have been that very night that his ghost started wandering through his home. Mariette DeAngelis, with a straight face and convincing tone, claims she hears him now, more than a century later, on dark moonless nights.

The DeAngelises, Mariette and John, started coming to Kennebunkport eight summers ago. On Mrs. DeAngelis's first ride into Kennebunk from the Port she noticed a dilapidated house on the corner of Summer Street and the Sea Road. "It has possibilities," she told herself. The house was a shell. Time and weather and vandals had sagged its shutters, torn up floor boards, flaked the paint; had splintered window panes and spread a wild profusion of weeds. But Mariette saw a vision of what it could be with a little imagination and a lot of work. She let the thought gestate.

The second summer, she made her way through tangled underbrush and peered through the shattered panes. The third summer she got her husband to look. The fourth year they bought the property and started restoration. Then they began to uncover its history.

Abial Kelley, trader, had bought the land from a Dimon Hubbard in 1793 and began building the house. In 1794 he moved in and after many years sold it to Dr. Swett—he of the fatal thirst—for $800. The eleven-room house became a hotbed of quarreling, the Swetts being none too amiable. They had come from Saccarappa (Scraparappa, a wit called it) to Kennebunk in 1844. Dr. Swett started out as a Free Will Baptist minister but changed his career to that of physician. It appears to have been a complete metamorphosis: he abandoned religion entirely and took to drink. The record hints at "unhappiness at home" as the cause. It also tells of "drunken brawls disturbing their neighbors." The doctor had a few friends who thought well of him but people generally were repelled by his manner and his practice dwindled. There were reports too that his morals "in another respect" were not good. The Swetts had "at least" five children. All but one died.

It was a gray dawn that fateful day when Jane Swett sent a girl of fourteen, an adopted daughter, out to the stable to search for the whisky she knew was hidden there. When the girl returned her mother uncorked the bottle and poured in forty grains of morphine. She then sent her back to the stable to hide the whisky where she had found it.

Later that morning, when Jane Swett saw her husband dying on the sofa in the living room, she herself took a large dose of morphine; so large, however, it acted as an emetic and she lived to stand trial. A local stomach pump, brought in to try to save the doctor, failed to function. Another was rushed from Biddeford but arrived too late. He died at 12:15 P.M.

The trial of Jane Swett began in Alfred on September 25, the same day that three doctors from Kennebunk and two from the Port performed a post-mortem on the victim's body, removing the stomach and sending it to Portland for examination. The lungs and other internal organs were in healthy condition except for a slight congestion in the brain. (The brain was weighed and found to be of more than average weight.) There seemed to be little doubt that the forty grains of morphine had proved a lethal dose.

On a rainy September 26th the doctor's funeral took place at his home. It could have been the weather that kept all but a few people from attending, but the doctor's friends, although loyal, were not numerous. The body was clothed in the doctor's best suit, and the face – usually dark skinned: "Indian blood," people said – appeared fresh as if alive. He was forty-eight. The town paid for the burial.

At the trial the defense took the stand that Mrs. Swett had not intended to kill her husband but only to "make him sick." ("Why, then," asked the judge, "didn't you give him ipecac?") On February 12 the jury brought in a verdict of manslaughter, a motion for a new trial was denied, and

Mrs. Swett was sentenced to the State Prison for six years. "People here," say the records in quaint understatement, "think she has been fortunate in not receiving a longer term in prison."

She was placed in a cell with two other women, one sentenced for horse stealing and the other to hang for murder. Put to work scrubbing and repairing the other convicts' clothes, she rebelled. She "would not," she told the deputy warden, "and should not put up with such accommodations and living." She had never been used to it. She was a landscape painter and it was important that her hands be kept free from such ruinous work.

Jane Swett was either very appealing or made life hell until she got what she wanted, because she was allowed liberties denied the other prisoners. Permission was granted, for example, for her to return home to fetch such furniture and articles as she wanted to make her cell livable; her life in jail seems to have contained all the elements of comfort except freedom.

Perhaps her ghost too now roams the Abial Kelley house. And perhaps she and the doctor are sometimes joined by another—a milder, sweeter little ghost—who wanders nostalgically through the rooms that were his home for three-quarters of a century. Henry Sargent, carriage painter (the fragmentary stencilling found on the walls was thought to have been his work), was the last occupant of the Kelley house before its long years of vacancy until the present owners took over. Frail and alone, he matched the slow decay of the house with his own. But he was content, dreamily living out his days in the rooms, now silent, that had once held so much hate and violence.

The day came when relatives decided he could no longer care for himself. He should be in a home for the aged. And the night before a niece was to collect him for this last journey, Henry Sargent walked out of the house he loved and into the stable, as the doctor had done—not for whisky, though, but to hang himself.

The three ghosts don't bother Mariette and John DeAngelis, who feel that the house belongs more to its past than to them. In a sense they have restored it for its earlier owners, combing local auctions for antiques which indeed could have been used—sat in, slept in, eaten from—by the unhappy doctor and his wife, or by Abial Kelley and Henry Sargent.

The house has eight fireplaces, seven of them dug out by the DeAngelises from behind decades of boards and layered wallpapers. There is a small opening behind one of the chimneys through which children could be pushed into a room beyond, to hide and keep warm during Indian attacks. A stone cistern covered by a trapdoor in the kitchen floor furnished water in housebound winters; and back of one of the closets an abandoned smoke room still bears the hooks that once held hams. Ceiling beams have been uncovered in three of the rooms. One bedroom is floored with boards found in the attic; the others boast the original wide floorboards.

The Kelley house, besides witnessing Kennebunk's first "civilized" murder (Indian and primitive murders don't count in this story), was the first to burn kerosene in a lamp. On Saturday nights, for half an hour, neighbors were invited in to see this wondrous sight. Nowadays electric switches supply a happy anachronism, flooding the spacious old rooms with a light never dreamed of by their early occupants.

But when the switches turn off the light, time turns back. Quiet descends on the ancient house, and suddenly a rocker may be set in motion and as suddenly cease . . . a small murmur comes from the old Indian hiding room . . . in the deep silence that follows, a floorboard creaks and a drapery at the window shimmers briefly in the moonless night.

It is at these times that the Abial Kelley house is returned to its ghosts.

The Adam McCulloch House

November 1, 1962

His presence haunts this room tonight
A form of mingled mist and light
From that far coast.
Welcome beneath this roof of mine!
Welcome! this vacant chair is thine,
Dear guest and ghost!

Robert Burns

ON AN AFTERNOON in the autumn of 1776 Adam McCulloch stood at the window of a back room in his house in Arundel. He appeared to be staring intently at the far rim of rolling land that stretched, unbroken by other habitation, around him. But he was not aware of the countryside; his eyes turned inward in his thoughts.

He was remembering a moment, just two days past, when through this same window he had watched the mob of townspeople, carrying torches, rush toward his house. Adam knew anger when he saw it. Back in Scotland he had known it in men like himself who had seen their land (tilled by them for so many generations they felt it belonged more to them than to the Dukes of Sutherland who leased it) confiscated for a hunting preserve.

But the Scotsmen's anger had availed them nothing. How many of them, Adam wondered, had sailed to the new world? How many, he thought — turning now from the window to gaze, satisfied, about him — had not only weathered the transplanting but thrived on it?

Frowning, he turned again to look through the window. His transplanting after all had not been a complete success. Some of his roots, so painfully cut, had been left back in beloved Scottish soil. He was like a man whose nerve-ends on the stump of an amputated leg still send pain down its absent length. He remembered thinking, watching the crowd draw nearer, that this pain and love must have invaded his face, to be seen by those who suspected in their friends and neighbors even a trace of old loyalty to the king.

The mob had stormed up to the house, their blazing torches held high for its timbers, and Adam—striding through the rooms, pausing for a reassuring word to Louisa who was gathering the children around her in the parlor—had thrown open the front door. "Some man among ye step forth!" he shouted. "Tis with one man only will I talk. Not the lot of ye, not angered as ye are."

A lad at the back was pushed through the crowd like a bucket in a fire brigade and stood scratching his shirt in shyness before Adam. Stuttering, he told of hearing whispered words of a secret room hereabouts, reached by a hidden staircase, where at any time of day or night might be found a spy in the pay of hated King George. And who but Adam had a house so built that it might hold a secret room?

When the boy finished, an angry murmur rose in the crowd. Adam held up his hand. "Secret room? Secret staircase?" He laughed and stood aside, waving his arm toward the open door behind him. "I invite ye, one and all," he said, "to examine my house. Look under beds, under rugs, for trapdoors. Knock on my walls. A hollow sound, ye well know, means a hidden chamber. My cellar, too. Don't forget that many a spy has come to a damp, inglorious end in Tory cellars."

The crowd stared silently up at him. This was Adam McCulloch, a man they liked. A man who had thrown in his lot with them, given them work in his shipyard, made friends among them. Would he so openly pave the way for discovery when it meant death or, at best, banishment? Hesitantly, they looked at one another. Adam saw heads shaking, caught the worried glances, the whispered consultations. Finally, a man stepped forward.

"We want no trouble, Adam," he said. "T'was not our wish to harm ye, only to make certain no aid was given the enemy. We'll only put ye under bond on your promise ye'll do naught to hurt the cause of liberty."

No one could see the muscles between Adam's shoulder blades relax nor the slight tremble of his knees. "T'will not concern me," he said, "to hold to a promise already kept."

Adam, looking now across the open field, noticed a small movement at the rim of the distant woods. It ceased. He searched for it a moment longer before his memories again took command. He was still deep in thought when he became aware of a slight rustle outside the door behind him.

Then came a knock.

It was nearing four o'clock of a bleak Thursday afternoon in the autumn of 1947. Phebe, wife of Keith Marshall, Adam McCulloch's great-great grandson, stood at the sink in her laundry preparing food for her five Scottish terriers. From time to time she glanced out the window at the land that rolled gently across fields and road to neighboring houses. Twilight lamps had begun to glimmer. Muffled by wet, fallen leaves, the cars on the road past the front of the house sounded like gusts of wind, gathering force as they approached and dying in the distance. Except for this and a slight scuffling noise made by the dogs at play, the house was silent.

She was alone. Her husband would be returning in an hour. Josephine, their housekeeper, had gone out. Phebe glanced through the window toward their neighbor's house, out of sight and some distance away. The Merrills would be preparing their supper, perhaps already sitting down to it. They ate early, as people hereabouts were prone to do.

The house sank into complete silence as the dogs, tired from their play, stretched out, tongues lolling, eyes fixed on the preparations at the sink. Phebe spooned the last of the mixture into a dish. She washed her hands and dried them. She was just bending down to the dogs with their food when she heard the sound—a knock on the laundry shed door.

Instantly the dogs set up a furious barking and raced toward the door. Suddenly, as if an unseen hand had gripped their throats, their barking stopped and they slid to a dead stop a few feet from the door. Seemingly paralyzed by something they alone could see, they stood transfixed, their eyes glued on the door, their hackles rising. Puzzled, Phebe walked past them. "It's only Uncle Chet," she told them. Smiling, she opened the door.

No one. Only the blackness of the shed met her eyes. She looked about, half expecting a neighbor to jump out and startle her with the prank. She went to the outer door and stepped into the twilight gloom. One neighbor only would have come on foot; she would have heard a car in the driveway. There was no car. She ran to the back of the house and looked down the path used by Chet or Grace Merrill on brief, friendly visits to bring a glass of homemade preserves or vegetables from their garden. The path was empty.

She decided not to mention the episode to Josephine. There was no need to scare her with something probably only imagined. But at dinner that night she told her husband and they laughed together over the dogs' strange, comical behavior.

The next morning she called on the Merrills. "Did either of you pay me a visit yesterday about four-thirty?" she asked. "Someone knocked on the laundry door but by the time I reached it . . . " She paused.

"No-o-o," Chet said slowly. "We haven't been over for about two weeks."

"Well, then, we have a ghost."

The Merrills looked at each other then back at Josephine.

"But it's a friendly ghost," Phebe went on. "I wasn't a bit frightened."

The following Friday morning, a week later: "What do you think, Josephine," Phebe said, "the Millers paid me a call yesterday afternoon." She smiled at Josephine's questioning look. "Oh, I know, they often drop over for a few minutes. But yesterday they came just at their supper time and stayed over an hour. What do you make of that?"

Josephine was ironing, her head bent over her work. "They didn't want you to be frightened."

"Frightened? Of what, for heaven's sake?"

"You know what I mean."

"Josephine! Don't tell me you know about our ghost?"

Josephine folded a towel methodically before she looked up. "I've known for a long time," she said. "Once when I was alone here I heard a knock on the door. I opened it, but nobody was there."

"The dogs . . . ?"

"Now Mrs. Marshall, I know those dogs are smart, but they can't knock on a door. Anyway, they were all inside, waiting for their dinner, and when the knock came they started for the door and then stopped and just stared, and when I opened it they whined like crazy."

Adam McCulloch came from Scotland in 1760 to settle in Arundel. He built ships on the banks of the Kennebunk River and built a house, on what is now the Old River Road, on two and a half acres bought from an early Merrill whose forebears had been granted title to the land during the reign of William and Mary.

Adam moved into his new house with his bride, Louisa Brown (her wedding gown is kept in perfect condition by descendants), and when children came he added an ell to the house—the community lacking a school—and taught his own and neighbors' children until a minister came to town who took over this function. But the ell was used as a schoolroom until well into the nineteenth century.

The Marshalls had acquired the property in 1937 but did not move in for several years. In 1930 William Barry, local architect, in casual conversation with them had mentioned his conviction that the spy stories of the McCulloch house were true. How had he determined this? There was a section, he said, whose windows were arranged most peculiarly and whose walls yielded a hollow sound when tapped. Also, stories of ghosts in the house had come down among the neighbors' families from Revolutionary times. And wasn't it rumored that the last occupant, a widow, would never enter the back part, claiming it was haunted? This, while interesting to the Marshalls, in time was forgotten.

In 1945 they moved in and began making the house habitable for year-round living. They decided to include the ell schoolroom in their plans, which meant cutting through what seemed an unusually thick wall in order to join the schoolroom to the rest of the second floor.

One morning the sound of hammers stopped. A shout brought the Marshalls running up the stairs. Facing them was a space four feet wide running the width of the house, a blank wall beyond, and remnants of what had been a floor.

The excitement of finding an area that could be converted into a bathroom and a closet won out over the Marshalls' feelings for antiquity (it wasn't until later they remembered the story of the secret room) and the workmen were directed to cut a door at the other end of the space. A while later, once again there came the sudden silence and a shout. This time the remains of three steps were discovered, leading downward.

Adam McCulloch lies entombed with his wife in a small cemetery near the house he built. He died in 1812, far from his native land.

Did his house harbor British spies?

And do their ghosts, seeking refuge, still creep through woods and over rolling land to knock on its door?

The Moses Paul House

October 28, 1970

MOSTLY IT WAS men working the soil, in the early days of our country, who built and lived in the ancient houses still to be seen in our Maine coastal towns. The houses were square, usually five rooms upstairs and five down, and there was no nonsense about them. Later, high ceilings and spacious rooms would come, and the wide-paned windows for more leisurely dwellers. In the early houses a man could reach up and touch the ceilings of rooms built small for warmth. He peered – for visitors, sometime for Indians or bears – through narrow windows with tiny panes that allowed a minimum of cold (or arrows?) to enter. Square and solid, the old homes enfolded the families living in them. In the woods outside, in the fields even, lurked danger. Inside the house were warmth and safety, and a closeness of family life that rarely has been known since in this land.

To such a house, built in 1780 in Eliot, one day in autumn twenty years ago came a couple seeking a retirement home. The realtor who had brought Rear Admiral and Mrs. Herbert Knowles to the empty building unlocked the door. He motioned them inside, but he himself remained on the doorstep. The house, he explained, was haunted.

"It was the most unpromising day imaginable," recalls Mrs. Knowles. "Rainy, misty, dreary. The talk about ghosts didn't disturb us, though. We had never given ghosts a thought. To us it was just a way of making conversation."

They took their time going through the rooms of the Old Moses Paul house. Its stanchions were firm, they noted, its beams honey colored with age. It was in a state of utter disrepair, however; fireplaces would have to be dug out from behind boards and plaster, a partition removed for the larger rooms that present-day heating systems made feasible. But the house was on a rise, nestled in flowering bushes and shade trees, and the Knowleses looked through small window panes onto a view that sloped into meadows and misted woodlands.

They bought the Old Moses Paul House and settled down to their retirement. Rooms upstairs were turned into a large workroom where the Admiral could make his ship models, sanding and polishing the fragments of wood until the finished craft gleamed like a jewel. Helen Knowles, who had attended the Maryland Institute of Art, at last had time to paint and to work on community projects. The slow turn of the Maine year, its seasons of activity and its seasons of rest, delighted them. Their days were spent at work, their evenings by themselves or with a few friends. They retired early, usually to read in bed in the cozy bedroom they shared on the ground floor. Had it been said this house was haunted? Nonsense.

The Knowleses had lived in the house for ten years. One early morning Helen Knowles opened her eyes. (She was to say later, "There is a twilight zone, just as you wake and just as you go to sleep, an interim that invites psychic things.") She was aware that a man was standing between her bed and her husband's. His clothes were of an earlier day—a white shirt of fine material, its full sleeves caught in at the wrists; he wore dark breeches, dark hose. His blue-black hair was long, touching his collar.

He started to walk toward the opposite wall. When he reached a long mirror that hung on the closet door, Helen Knowles screamed. The man swung around and smiled at her. His complexion, she saw, was olive, his eyes shining and as black as his hair. He turned—and disappeared through the mirror.

Mrs. Knowles was shaken, but not unpleasantly so. There had been a gentleness, a charm that eased fear except for the startled moment of her scream. Her husband had been awakened by the scream and she discussed the episode with him. They put it down as a dream, a dream that had seemed more real to her than most. Gradually they forgot about it.

Then small happenings began to occur. One night the Knowleses lingered over coffee in their dining room with a friend. The Admiral left the table for a moment; his wife went for more coffee. From the kitchen she heard her friend call: "Helen! Come quick. There's a red ball of light. It's playing around the ceiling beams!"

Another night the Admiral had turned off the light over his bed and Mrs. Knowles was about to do the same when suddenly there appeared above them the ball of red light. It traveled around the ceiling for a few moments, landed on the bureau and faded away. What had it been? A flashlight from outside? Automobile headlights? The shape and color and movement of the ball were such that neither of these possibilities was acceptable. Nor did any other explanation occur to them.

A friend whom Mrs. Knowles describes as highly psychic, was sitting with the Knowleses around the fireplace in their living room one night when she suddenly stared fixedly at a Victorian sofa at the far end of the room. "Somebody is sitting there," she said. "She is terribly upset. She used to love the stairs in this house. She doesn't like the way you've changed them."

Again, in the kitchen one day Helen Knowles felt a form brush against her. "Excuse me," she said involuntarily, and turned around. No one was there.

These episodes were intriguing to the Knowleses who had never before had a psychic experience. They made for a tingling of the spine, a feeling of hair rising on the backs of their necks. But it was not until they had lived in the house for seventeen years that something happened to make Helen Knowles remember her ghostly vision of seven years before.

One evening their host at the Pepperell Mansion in Kittery Point mentioned that the Old Moses Paul House had once given asylum to a refugee during the French Revolution. The Knowleses pondered this. Was it the spirit of the refugee that Helen Knowles had seen? The phantom in eighteenth century clothes that had walked, like Alice in Wonderland, through the looking glass?

It is 1968. Mrs. Knowles is compiling and illustrating a booklet for a tour she has organized of historic homes in Eliot. "Twice Told Tales" is to tell of old Eliot as its people remembered stories passed down to them, or as written records and tales were found in desks and attics. One day Gladys Paul, a descendant of the Pauls who had built and lived in the Old Moses Paul House, brought to Mrs. Knowles an excerpt a relative had discovered in *Sprague's Journal of Maine History*, a compilation, now out of print, of journals published in the early twentieth century in Dover-Foxcroft, Maine. The account had been written by a Melvil F. Meeds, great-great-grandson of Moses Paul:

One snowy night in the early winter of 1794, on top of a high hill in the little town of Eliot, a big, friendly, rambling farmhouse with spacious rooms and cozy fireplaces, sent its beckoning beacon of light far across the fields towards the shores of the Piscataqua. To the traveler straying from his road at dusk, it was indeed a haven of refuge, for in those days, every man's house was open to the traveler, so that the latchstring was always out, and at this homestead of my great-grandfather's, Moses Paul, it was not unusual at twilight, for some stranger to beg a bed on the floor in front of the open fire for the night, thus causing the lady of the house no inconvenience.

On this particular night of which my great-grandmother told this tale, the supper and chores were over and the family assembled around the fire. In one corner sat Madame Paul, as she was called, knitting and nodding. On the other side sat the master of the house by the little candlestand, while sprawled upon the floor, his face nearly in the blaze, was the son, Hugh (my future grandfather), a lad of fourteen, doing his "sums" on a shovel, to be corrected by Master Jordan, a King's surveyor, when next he passed that way.

Into this peaceful silence of home life came a faint fumbling, as of a latch lifted but yet not enough to open. Young Hugh quickly raised his head with "An Indian?" for in those days, the tales of Indians and bears told by the fathers were so vivid that every strange sound might, to the young imagination, prove to be either. On going to the door, Mr. Paul started back as a form fell in across the floor. Dragging the unconscious youth to the fire, he tried to arouse him, but with a muttered "Mon Dieu" the youth sank into a deep stupor. It was evident that this unknown guest was sick and exhausted. He was not like the men of those days, as he was dressed in the tatters of what was once a smart French uniform, but now it was so soiled and torn that it barely covered him.

. . . Madame Paul helped put the sick man to bed. For days she nursed him through the fever and delirium, which was full of mutterings of French, of which they were ignorant, except when uttering the word "America," then he would give a sigh of relief and doze peacefully for a few minutes as if he realized he was safe in the arms of that sought-for haven.

On recovering, he made known his wish to work his board for he evidently had no intention of leaving. So they gave him light work around the place, but the poor lad had never worked, as was shown by his hands, small, delicate, white and soft as a girl's. Valiantly he tried to do his share, for in those days of hardships, he who ate must work. The farmer lads rather despised him for his frail efforts to split wood and carry heavy burdens, but his French courage never faltered and he did his part. He gave as his name, (Enri) Henry. The most noticeable thing about him was his court manners where ladies were; when any of the women entered the room, he always rose and remained standing till they were seated. If they dropped anything, he sprang to pick it up; but the most unusual of all was when he retired at night, he always bowed to all, then dropping on one knee in front of Madame Paul, he would kiss her hand.

About a year after he came, three men in uniform rode into the yard on horseback and asked "if a Frenchman worked there." The little daughter went to the field to summon Henry, who was helping with the harvesting. When Henry came into the house, the men bowed from the waist and saluted him in his own language. One of them drew a long official envelope with a coat of arms on it from his breast pocket and presented it to Henry. Henry read it, then tore it to bits and tossed the bits into the fireplace. With shoulders back and heels together, he snapped a command to them in French. They saluted him, sprang on to their horses and were off down the steep hill towards Portsmouth, and Henry, saying not a word of explanation to the amazed family, quietly went back to his harvesting.

A few weeks later, on calling him to breakfast, it was found he had gone, leaving a note in broken English thanking them for their hospitality, ending, "I go to my La Belle France."

And this is the tale of the French refugee who took shelter from no one knows what perils across in France. It was always supposed that he was landed by a small boat in Portsmouth harbor and rowing up the river landed on the Eliot side and seeing the bright welcoming light at Great-Grandfather Paul's on the high hill, walked the dreary, snowy road, wet and exhausted, with his eye ever on the beacon of light, thinking of the warmth and comfort and protection he would find in this land so friendly to his own France, an exile yet in friendly hands, a mystery never to be solved.

Melvil F. Meeds

Helen Knowles, who now "scoffs at nothing," has this to say about ghosts: "It is my feeling that so-called ghosts are simply manifestations of those earth-bound souls who have departed to another plane and who wish to make themselves known to those of us who remain on this earth . . . 'Ghosts' are but a brief facet in the concepts of psychic phenomena, which include dowsing, clairvoyance, and many, many more phases of the occult and unseen forces of life."

The Kingsbury House

November 11, 1970

What beckoning ghost along the moonlight shade
Invites my steps and points to younder glade?

Alexander Pope

ELIZABETH BOURNE had been hearing the noise for several minutes and it was beginning to disturb her.

Not that she was easily disturbed, this woman. The seas kill your sea-captain husband and leave you with three young children; you marry a twice-widower with six of his own and then you and he have six more. This, in the pre-gadget days of our ancestors, could either make or break a woman. It had not broken Elizabeth Bourne and it would take more than a mysterious noise at the back of her house to do it now.

But husband John was on a business trip and she was alone with her small army of children. There was no way to communicate with the neighbors. And it was a bitterly cold moonlit night in midwinter when no one with ordinary business would be about.

In one of the children's bedrooms, she finished tucking in the last child, placing an extra quilt over him against the chill that poked drafty fingers into the room. He was half asleep. "Noise," he mumbled, his eyelids drooping, "what's that noise, mother?"

Elizabeth leaned down and kissed him. "It's only a loose chain in the barn, dear one. Go to sleep now." She rose, glanced at the other children asleep in the room and tiptoed out.

In the hall she heard the noise again, louder now and higher, as if, like a clumsy barnyard fowl, it had taken wing and soared to an upper window. Elizabeth opened the last children's bedroom and peeked in. They all were sleeping soundly. She closed the door softly and stood staring toward the back of the house.

The noise was very clear now. It was a clanking of metal and it was coming from outside a window in the back bedroom, a room used occasionally for friends or travelers. Outside the window was a roof covering a passageway that led from the kitchen to the barns. The roof was two feet below the window sill. Someone was standing on it. Someone was trying to get in.

Terror—for the children's safety—crept through Elizabeth. She started to run. Almost soundlessly she passed through the house toward the back, thinking as she went. How could she secure the window? Move the oaken chest against it? And if entrance were blocked at that window would the intruder start forcing another? She could not spend the night pushing, with failing strength, heavy pieces of furniture against windows. Pausing, she snatched a piece of firewood from the bin. At least she would have a weapon.

She reached the door of the bedroom and swung it open. The room was ice cold and black, but the moon shone on a glinting ice world outside. At the window, exhaling a mist that fogged its outlines, was a huge shape.

Elizabeth shut the door and felt her way to the mantel. Trembling, she lit a candle and holding it high she approached the window. Seen clearly now, the huddled shape took the form of a man. Tangled hair fell to his shoulders and a matted beard climbed to eyes that stared back at her, dull, unblinking. The man slowly raised his arms, flattening his palms against the window panes. His wrists were manacled.

She turned and ran to the table where she held her sputtering candle to a whale-oil lamp. Holding tight the piece of firewood, she returned to the window, pressed the releases, then ran to the door and stood with her back to it. Barely breathing, the firewood grasped in both hands, she watched the window slowly open. The man swung a leg over the sill and paused to look sideways at her. He pulled the other leg in and stood like a bull about to charge, his head lowered, his curiously dead eyes focused on the door behind her. Suddenly he scuttled crabwise into a far corner, beyond the reach of the lamp's beams. He sank to the floor and began to curl in on himself until he formed almost a fetal ball.

Elizabeth ran to the window, slammed it shut. Whirling, she made for the fireplace and thrust in shavings and kindling. She lit them, fanning until a blaze sprang up. After a moment's hesitation, she threw in the piece of firewood clutched in her hand and then flexing her palms—the bark had cut into them cruelly—she was out of the room and back in an instant with more firewood. To the kitchen then where she poured a bowl of the hot soup kept simmering in an iron pot at the back of the stove. She cut a thick piece of bread and, running back upstairs, set the food on the floor. "Eat," she commanded.

The man's imprisoned hands grabbed the bread. He tore at it with his teeth, swallowing chunks of it whole. Then, grasping the hot pewter that held the soup, he jerked back in pain. Elizabeth knelt down and picking up the ladle started to feed him. He sucked the hot brew into his mouth in great burning gulps.

Elizabeth was close to him, so close that scars of mistreatment were revealed to her. Only then did she let herself feel overwhelming compassion. (He had escaped, she learned afterward, from an insane asylum. He was not dangerous, although why harmless lunatics should not turn into dangerous ones at the treatment meted out to them — living worse than animals, starved, manacled, chained in their own filth — Elizabeth did not know. Wandering through the fields and woods of Kennebunk in the bitter cold, he had seen the lighted house, was trying to open the window when Elizabeth found him.)

He stretched out his back onto the floor. He was fed now, and warm, but the firelight was merciless, exposing to Elizabeth's shocked eyes the matted hair, the scraps of rags he wore as clothes, the haggard lines of his ravaged face. As she watched, he turned on his side, pillowed his cheek on the manacled hands and sighed once, deeply, like a child. Almost at once he was asleep.

Elizabeth looked pityingly down on him a moment longer, then seating herself in a rocker between the sleeping man and the door she prepared for a night vigil.

The Kingsbury House would gladly boast of the ghost of Elizabeth Bourne if it could. But isn't it only the unhappy, unfulfilled lives that return as ghosts, trying through eternity to settle unfinished business?

So it can't be Elizabeth's ghost that dwelt long ago in the small closet under the front stairway of the Kingsbury house. The ghost anyway was exorcised by seven ministers praying outside the closet for seven days and seven nights.

Nor can it be her ghost that still climbs behind you up the back stairs (and no further), endlessly mounting toward something wanted but never attained.

Nor could it be the ghost of any of the fifteen Bourne children, those cherished ones who tumbled about the large house, busy as bees with cooking and weaving and games and books.

Nor Abigail, who at seventeen sent to Dolly Madison the handwoven counterpane, charmingly embroidered:

Beneath [sic] this bed
illustrious pair repose,
Secure from foreign
and domestic foes.
May white plumed seraphs
watch around this bed,
And Heaven
its kindlier influences shed.

So pleased was Dolly Madison that she wrote her gratitude to Abigail and enclosed a gold ring and chain;

Nor Sukey, who thriftily "spun her stockings in the evenings";

Nor Edward, who became a judge and author of *Bourne's History of Kennebunk and Wells;*

Nor Julia Ann who "was fully versed in the science of domestic economy; the culinary operations were at her fingers' end; so that when a husband should need [for anything] she would not be at her wit's end to know what to do."

Julia Ann married Henry Kingsbury in 1825, thus passing the Lyman House to the Kingsbury line which has occupied it for five generations. Henry, great-grandfather of Theodore, the present owner, was born in 1801 in York. At ten he decided that God had meant him to see the world, so he went to Wiscasset, ostensibly to visit an older brother but really to remove himself from parental veto so he could live his own life. The records follow him prosaically—precosity must have been the order of the day—through adventures seldom befalling mature men, much less a ten-year-old.

He shipped himself to Liverpool, spending several months there and returned to Wiscasset where he enlisted on a privateer (this was during the War of 1812). Hardly out at sea, the privateer was chased by a British frigate and sought safety in Boston harbor. Young Henry's courage and seamanship so impressed naval authorities there that they offered him the office of midshipman. This would have made him boss of several men—he was older now, eleven—and we can imagine his chagrin when his father firmly ordered him home, thus nipping in the bud a promising nautical career. In due time he settled down as the husband of Julia Ann to an earthbound life of partnership with one of her brothers as a builder of ships. In 1850 he was irrevocably anchored as a landsman when he became a member of the House of Representatives.

No, we have to let these early occupants of the Kingsbury House rest in peace. Rather can we say the restless ghost is Theodore Lyman himself, builder of the magnificent addition to father-in-law Emerson's simple house—so beautiful that in the 1780s visitors from abroad came to see it. So haunted that in 1939 a caretaker said, "I know men who wouldn't spend one night in this house."

When he was twenty-three, Theodore Lyman married Sarah, sole survivor and legatee of Waldo Emerson (uncle of Ralph). Sarah, along with her tender years—she was fourteen and a half when she married—brought considerable property to Theodore, who was ambitious. If riches bring happiness then Sarah must have lived in a crescendo of joy as her husband's Midas touch brought money into his coffer. We have the facts of Theodore's profitable West India and China trade, his acquisition of more and more property, his astute business practices. It may be that Sarah, at twenty-one, died of an excess of happiness. More likely she succumbed to one of the diseases that filled old-time cemeteries with children and young adults. Their two babies died too, one at eight days, the other at two years. Theodore was left alone.

It was then that he started improving his house, making it so magnificent that one distinguished visitor wrote in his diary, " . . . It is fit for a nobleman, and I have seen nothing like it in this country, and scarcely anywhere."

Theodore must have rattled around in it, though, because two years after Sarah's death he brought home a bride he'd found among Salem's aristocracy. Possibly the new Mrs. Lyman was bored in Kennebunk. We can imagine life in the large house, with a husband wedded to business interests, to have had its moments of ennui. Whatever the reason, four years later found them in Waltham where Theodore ended his days at eighty-six in an even larger, grander residence and with a top-heavy fortune. He never returned to Kennebunk.

Is this the life of a man who was happy? Perhaps. We'll never know.

But it could be the ghost of Theodore Lyman that mounts endlessly the back steps of the house he built. What— promising release but never yielding it—beckons him at the top of the stairs? Is it a long-ago moment of true happiness, a fleeting movement he ignored? Perhaps a shy trusting caress from the child that was his bride? Does he climb through eternity to capture this lost moment?

Or is it the ghost of a manacled human who seeks forever to relive his one lone night of warmth and safety, long ago in the Kingsbury house?

The Caleb Emery House

December 9, 1970

I hear, far off, at some forgotten door,
A music and an eerie faint carouse,
And stir of echoes down the creaking floor."

Archibald MacLeish

HAUNTED HOUSES creak and groan. Occasionally they screech or whimper. Rarely do they play a guitar.

One night the children now living in the old Caleb Emery House in Eliot had gone to bed. Their mother was in the master bedroom upstairs. Their father, working in a room at the back of the house, heard the sound of a guitar. A guitar was kept standing in a corner of the living room, but his wife was upstairs and the children were in bed. Who could be plucking at the strings?

He started walking toward the living room and the sound stopped. "Mary Ann," he called upstairs to his wife. "Are you there?"

"Yes."

"Were you strumming the guitar?"

"No, I thought you were."

Bill Bailey continued on to the living room. The guitar was in its usual place. He put his ear to the strings; there was no vibration. "The cat," he decided. He looked around the room but no cat was to be seen. He went to the front door and opened it. Out of the night the cat came at him, bounding across the threshold to rub itself against his legs.

Who, unseen, gently rocked this chair at night? / Photo by the author, 1970

The house, built in 1814 in the high-ceilinged, spacious style of some early nineteenth century homes by Dr. Caleb Emery for his bride, Mary Ann Carpenter, looks huge for its only nine rooms. I am sitting with Mary Ann Bailey in the living room. The room is decorated comfortably with family heirlooms, including oils of Bill's ancestors that lend a mellow luster to the atmosphere of antiquity. The Bailey cat rests on the hearth. Bailey children — there are three — run in from time to time to lean their elbows in their mother's lap, as children do unconsciously to assure themselves all is well.

"The guitar thing happened twice," Mary Ann is saying. "The second time exactly the same as the first. Each of us thought the other was playing it. There are feelings in this room," she went on. "It has the sense of fullness, more than what we build into it. I wish I knew about Caleb's and Mary Ann's lives. I feel their lives just by living here. It is a happy house. 'Good vibes,' as they say. I don't have a strong belief in ghosts, but I'm willing to believe in them if they're around. I have no fear of them. No, I love this room. It is very free."

Mary Ann's major in college was anthropology. After graduation she went to India for a year, to the University of Bombay, to do research on Gandhi. "I was interested from the nonviolence standpoint. I wanted to see what made it work once. Wouldn't it be great if it could work again somewhere?"

She returned home to join the Laboratory of Human Development at Harvard. She met and married Bill, and later they came to Eliot to live. Bill is an analyst programmer for the University of New Hampshire.

"It's interesting," she was saying now. "I am Mary Ann too, like Caleb's wife. And two of my children have the same names as two of hers — William and Elizabeth, only the first Elisabeth was spelled with an 's'. And I never knew about the Emerys till we moved here."

"What tune did the guitar play?" I asked.

"No tune. It made rather timid noises. Quite gentle."

The guitar playing was not the only psychic phenomenon the Baileys have experienced in the Caleb Emery house. When a friend, a divinity student, was visiting them the three were sitting in the living room one night after the children had gone to bed. They were relaxed, sometimes talking, just sitting silently and gazing into the flames of the wood fire ablaze on the hearth.

The fireplace is opposite two doors, one of which is in the corner nearest the front hallway. Bill was sitting on the left of the hearth, the visiting friend opposite him. In the three-way conversation they looked often toward Mary Ann who sat between the two doors on a sofa across the room from them. Suddenly their voices stopped, and their eyes became riveted on a misty figure that had appeared in the doorway leading into the hall. "No one said anything." (Mary Ann is telling me about it.) "I didn't see the figure. I was facing away from the door; it was out of my range of vision. It just stood there for what seemed several minutes, then it melted away."

"Do you ever try to materialize these figures?" I asked Mary Ann.

"No. How do you do that?"

Another time a friend gifted with extrasensory perception was visiting them. Once as she was mounting the stairs in the front hall she gave a sudden jump. "What's the matter?" asked Bill from the bottom of the stairs.

"A cat just brushed past me, a white cat."

There is no white cat in the Bailey household. But far in the past there had been. "An old carpenter — Murray Rowe, he's still alive — had turned some of the floors for Elisabeth Bartlett who owned the house later. He remembers a white Angora cat."

In the fourth, and so far the last, episode nothing was seen or heard, only sensed. Scott Parkin, who until recently was on the staff of the *Star*, was sitting with the Baileys one summer night in their living room. "The windows were wide open," he recalls, "but the doors to the room were closed. It was stormy outside — that may have been it — but all of a sudden there was a pressure in the room. It was weird. I've never had that sensation before. The feeling that something is there with you and you don't know what it is."

Dr. Caleb Emery was the son of William Emery of Sanford and grandson of Colonel Caleb Emery of Eliot and Sanford. "One of the most prominent men of his time," old Eliot records have it, "of more than local reputation as a skillful physician and business man . . . who began the practice of medicine in Eliot, and continued the same till his death . . . Dr. Emery was a man of great personal magnetism; of strict integrity; and marked force of character.

"He took a great interest in the welfare of his State, and was a leader in political circles . . .

"He is said to have been a remarkably handsome man, about 5′10″ in height, and rather stout.

"His death . . . [cast] a deep gloom in the community; and no man has ever left more warm personal friends. Dr. Emery was a gifted speaker, and delivered many . . . orations . . . "

From a William Fogg's journals of the time (one of the entries: "Tuesday, May 3, 1814, in the forenoon I assisted Dr. Emery raise his house-frame") we see the ubiquitous and handsome Caleb darting about Eliot as physician answering calls of the sick; as Collector of the Town; as appraiser for the will of "Jane Frost, Gentlewoman;" as justice of the peace for York County; as school committee member; as one of three men to sell "the privilege for a pew on the east end of the old men's seats, joining the broad aisle" of his church. We see him as treasurer at the annual town meeting on April 9, 1820. ("The Meeting was very large and very noisy, and continued from 10 o'clock in the morning to 7 o'clock in the evening.")

We see him holding in his home "a meeting of the Revolutionary Soldiers of Eliot . . . to give deposition . . . to get their names on the Pension List under a late Act of Congress . . . " We notice his signature, one of fourteen, beseeching the selectmen of the town of Eliot in a communication dated September 6, 1814: " . . . We the subscribers, freeholders and residents of the town of Eliot, viewing our frontier as being in danger of an attack from the enemy, and believing we are not in that state of preparation which we ought to be for the common defense request you to call a Town Meeting . . . "

Before his speeches Caleb, like Lincoln, was prone to use any handy piece of paper for his thoughts. On the blank leaf of a letter dated July 1, 1825, he jots the name of Lafayette and scrawls notes for an oration he is to give on July 4 about a visit to New England of the colonies' most famous friend of the Revolution:

The past has been an eventful year. It brought to our shores LaFayette—the friend and companion of our Washington.

He came, and a whole Nation rose up to honor him.

He has traveled through the territories of these United Republics, he met the acclamations and blessings of the People. They have accorded to him honors as man never before received.

Europe has heard the sound of his triumph; and despots have trembled.

We can imagine Caleb's mellifluous voice three days later rolling out the impassioned oration that has come down to us in the records, ending with: "The voice of Washington that reached him [Lafayette] in the Austrian dungeon could not welcome him to the shades of Mt. Vernon. But the grateful children of America have bid him welcome in his name. Yes, every tongue hath exclaimed with emphasis and joy—Welcome Welcome Lafayette!"

Elsewhere in the records two other fragments of Dr. Emery's pen give a glance at his religious thought: "Nothing is more evident than that God has but ONE CHURCH in the world." And "Do not mistake impulse for the spirit of God."

Caleb and Mary Ann produced six children. The two oldest boys, Caleb and Chandler, went south while quite young and stayed there. Daughter Elisabeth married a "Mr. Vincent." Lydia did not marry. The youngest son, William, for years a draughtsman at Kittery Navy Yard, inherited the old homestead. (Where is the sixth child? I have not been able to discover what happened to it.)

A woman's participation in community affairs, if she did participate, was seldom mentioned in the old records. There is little in the prolific William Fogg's journals about Mary Ann. She was the Reverend Samuel Parson Chandler's oldest daughter. The names of her brothers and sisters, and their spouses if they married, are given. Mary Ann herself married Caleb on October 14, 1813. That's about all. These shadowy women no doubt baked, mended, tended the homes while their husbands built and maintained the villages, and generally led the colorful lives that fill pages of the old journals. (It might have been the "color" of his life that did Caleb in. He died of a heart attack when he was forty-three. He was running for governor at the time.)

Mary Ann lived to be eighty in the house her husband had built her. Their graves are some distance from the house, on what was once their property but is now owned by Central Maine Power Company. "We're worried," says the latter-day Mary Ann, "that they'll build a power plant over the graves."

After the son William Emery, James Coleman, a printer, became owner of the Caleb Emery House. The deed passed to him on July 18, 1898. Little is known about him, although he must have lived in the house for thirty-odd years. He sold it in the 1930s to Elisabeth Bartlett. Elisabeth lived there until her death in 1951. "She must have been a woman of some means," Mary Ann conjectures. "She didn't marry and she took to live with her a curious figure, Anna Vinton. They went to Europe several times and brought back beautiful things. Anna was several years younger than Elisabeth. She seemed to have had nothing of her own. She took care of her companion and when Elisabeth died inherited everything. She lived out her life alone in the house, tending her cats and seeing little of humanity."

When she died, the house and its contents went to Strawbery Banke which selected what it wanted for its restorations and put the rest up for auction. "We went to it. It was in September 1965 in Hampton, New Hampshire. We bought one item, a rocking chair. There it is." Mary Ann pointed to a corner of the living room where a small rocking chair sat facing a guitar.

Who is it that comes back? Who stands between the darkness of the hallway and a firelit room that murmurs with voices of companionship. Who sits, perhaps, in the little rocker and touches the strings of the guitar? Caleb Emery? No, he would be leaning over a town official's shoulder, injecting his spirit into town meeting. He would be fitting a ghostly harness on a horse to answer a sick call. He would hover over the paved roads of Eliot, he who planned in 1815 to protest at the next court of session on behalf of Eliot "the state of the road through the middle of the Town . . . " No, not Caleb.

It must be the women; or one of them. " . . . Timid," today's Mary Ann had said of the sound the guitar made that night. "Quite gentle."

7

The Environment

The "Clearwater" puts into port during a later cruise / Photo by the author, 1970

The Launching of the *Clearwater*

July 2, 1969

IN A SPANKING breeze, the *Clearwater* slid into the sea at South Bristol, Maine, at 12:30 P.M. on May 17th to the singing of upward of a thousand people who filled, and spilled out of, the enormous building that had housed the sloop in Gamage's shipyard.

Built to dramatize water pollution, the sloop is a replica of those sailing the Hudson River in the last century carrying passengers and freight on an aquatic lifeline that antedated the building of highways and railroads. The sails of these sloops billowed through an era that will never come again. But the man who dreamed *Clearwater* and the men and women who worked with him to make the dream come true aim that the era will not be forgotten—not its whipping canvases, the clean lines of its sloops nor the unpolluted waters the graceful craft sailed upon.

From the time the idea of the sloop took shape in the mind of folksinger Pete Seeger—through the moment when naval architect Cyrus Hamlin of Kennebunk first put pencil to drawing board and the Hudson River Sloop Restoration, Inc., was formed—to when *Clearwater* hit the water, the creation of the sloop had taken over three years.

There was little source material to draw on. The papers and pamphlets Cyrus Hamlin was able to collect measured only an inch thick. "This is about all there is," he says ruefully. "Except for *The Sloops of the Hudson* and some builders' half-models and occasional sailmakers' drawings, I don't think anything is extant from those days. Oh, there were some lines in a book, too, written in 1840 by a relative of Donald McKay who was the foremost clippership builder in the world."

There was this, there was a dim and ancient oil painting of a Hudson River sloop in the Smithsonian Institution, and there was a placemat that Cy's wife Jean had picked up somewhere showing an old schooner tied at a dock in Camden. From these slim sources, Hamlin put together on his drawing board one of the sleekest vessels ever to spread its canvas wings over water. There will be more. Poughkeepsie and other Hudson

River towns are thinking of building them, Harlem too. They too will be used in the interest of saving our waters from those who knowingly or unknowingly would destroy them. And a 34-foot catamaran for Millersville State College in Pennsylvania has been launched in Boothbay Harbor — it was present at *Clearwater*'s launching — and a similar craft will soon be started for the University of Maine.

Clearwater, a floating museum, will sail from South Bristol down to the Hudson to maneuver the same waters its ancestors did, putting into ports along the way so the public may know the ways the sloop hopes to combat pollution, and so it may see an example of a craftsmanship thought to be dying or dead.

"Shipyards generally have lost their ancient skills," said one of the speakers at *Clearwater*'s launching. "A search up and down the Hudson failed to yield one shipyard that could undertake the work. There just were no more of them." Then Maine's Harvey F. Gamage was found, a shipbuilder who still knew enough of the old craft to take on the job.

Gamage stayed away from the microphone during the ceremonies which took place under the prow of the sloop inside the building. "Too busy," he said laconically, continuing his check of details before the sloop would start down the ways. But Pete Seeger spoke, and played his guitar and sang. Governor Curtis spoke, and Cy Hamlin. Steven Rockefeller spoke ("only his South American tour prevented my father's being here today"), as well as several others who could hardly be heard — at least outside, where the commotion made loudspeakers set up for the occasion virtually useless.

A long, serpentine line of men, women and children, made ravenous by the brisk and tangy air, filed past a table bearing salads, bread, cheeses, pies, cakes and (alas) canned beverages. "We sent down one hundred twenty-five loaves of bread," said the local storekeeper, "forty-eight packages of celery, fifty bunches of carrots and twenty-five heads of lettuce." Many of the crowd, besides, had brought their own lunches.

The speeches began at 11:30, ended an hour later at the suspenseful moment when the sloop, held by cables and ropes, inched through the great open doors, was released, and rushed down the ways, entering the water with a mighty splash, the men aboard her scrambling over her decks in rapid and orderly confusion, manipulating their ropes like snake charmers. A cheer, and one of the most colorful launchings in Maine waters in our time was over.

The crowd began to make its way out of the building and out of the yard, toward its cars. As they left, a woman with a large plastic bag began to pick up the refuse left behind.

Left behind too — bobbing gently in waters that had so recently welcomed a sloop that will publicize pollution and filth — were paper cups, bottles, beer and soda cans, and sandwich wrappers.

Since her launching twenty-two years ago, a check-up of *Clearwater*'s investigative examination of New York's polluted Hudson River shows that spoilage dumped into the river can be decreased and ultimately ended. This, in spite of the fact that generations of dumping must still be dealt with to restore the river's pristine purity. Weather permitting, *Clearwater* makes daily trips on the Hudson. Her passengers are adults and children who while aboard take courses in sailing and navigation as well as learn of the Hudson's history and its biology. Interest in these study-cum-pleasure trips has reached the point where a sister sloop is contemplated to accommodate passenger overflow. The project is now under the aegis of Hudson River Sloop Clearwater, Inc., of Poughkeepsie.

Ten years ago Pete Seeger and Cy Hamlin planned what Seeger calls his "Hudson River Ferry Sloop." Two of these are already launched, another is under construction. The three are designed for clean-up and education while under sail and will take off from various points along the Hudson.

And what happened to all that trash strewn along the shore during the launching? When the crowd had dispersed, Seeger and Hamlin assembled a crew to shovel it (brought back to shore now by the incoming tide) into a large truck which landed several loads onto the town dump. Then all departed, leaving behind a spotless shoreline. To the old adage "waste not, want not" should be added "and trash not." We're fast running out of dumps.

Ecologs

January 6, 1971

THE UNSEEN FORCE of atomic radiation attacks us twenty-four hours a day. Fight back. Avoid all unnecessary X-rays. Agitate for safe methods of power production (solar, for example).

Nuclear fission's radioactivity cannot be wholly contained. It goes into the air and water at plant sites and fuel reprocessing plants. Worse, we all know about the hazardous journey high-level wastes take to their burial grounds where they require constant watch.

We must not allow *any* additional radiation into our environment. Because every addition means more leukemia, more cancer, more birth defects.

January 27, 1971

WE NOW NUMBER 200 million souls in the United States. Or 400 times as many as there were when nature was in balance.

We are wrecking the land and we continue to talk of progress in terms of *growth* – more of everything.

Practice population control before one of Nature's disasters or war controls it for us. Do not believe the misleading reports about a lowering United States birth rate. *The number of births still grows each year in the United States.*

Learn about starvation in India, China, Latin America, Africa, and don't think it can't happen here. An enlightened people will reduce its numbers.

February 10, 1971

THE WORLD is a vehicle spinning through space. It carries on it three and a half billion people dependent for their lives on a thin envelope of air. Neil Armstrong, first man on the moon, last November compared the world to an oasis or an island and said, "It is the only island that we know is a suitable home for man . . . Protection [of it] seems most required . . . from its own population."

A million American housewives can set in motion a trend that could literally save the world. It is not necessary to band together. Each can act on her own or in cooperation with her neighbors. And an interesting side benefit is: an individual family can save $500 or more a year.

How?

Key means of cutting through the enormous bulk of household waste are to (1) re-use and (2) become a small, instead of a large, consumer.

May 1971

SOFT DRINKS MAGAZINE has reported a sudden increase in demand for returnable bottles. *The Wall Street Journal* reports this too, but the *Journal* thinks such a demand will be short-lived unless women are serious about returning bottles.

Two big reasons for buying beverages in returnable bottles: (1) Our taxes, which are rising, include the mounting cost of collecting and disposing of those one-way bottles and cans you see strewn along our byways and highways. (2) Drinks in returnable bottles are cheaper.

Keep asking your market manager to stock returnable bottles. The reason you may be having trouble finding them is that retailers often consider them too much trouble to stock and handle. Try to convince your retailer that a cleaner environment may mean we're all inconvenienced somewhat, but that if women are willing to take the trouble to return bottles, retailers should be willing to supply them and take them back.

August 4, 1971

A STUDY OF governmental conservation programs, says ecologist Dr. Luc Hoffmann, has led to "extremely pessimistic conclusions." Official conservation efforts so far have produced only an "insignificant patchwork" compared with the "galloping degradation" of our environment.

"We must all now know," he says, "that the resources of the biosphere (the totality of man's environment) are finite and cannot be increased." He questions whether our earth can provide adequate life even for the present 3.5 billion world population. And the population is expected to increase to 6 billion in the next thirty years. "If it proves impossible to control population increase, the human race is doomed to early extinction."

In short, all you young people, the damage has been done by your elders in producing so many of you. It's up to you, now, to plan carefully the number of progeny you will be placing on our overcrowded globe.

September 1, 1971

PEOPLE CONTINUE doing things the old way out of habit. You and I do it. Organizations like clubs, universities, city halls and the federal government do it. But the time seems to be upon us to reassess what we do out of habit—our waste of paper for example.

All kinds of mail come to the *Star*—advertising, correspondents' copy, stories and news releases on recycled paper. Some continue to waste paper, like the U.S. Air Force, the Navy, and others that are apt to send a common news release as if it were a certificate to be framed.

One came this morning. It was a mimeographed sheet of paper whose blank spaces were filled in with the name and pertinent details of a York County man who has completed a tour of activity as an Air Force officer. It was sent in a large manila envelope and protected by corrugated cardboard. We measured and weighed it. It weighed one and three-quarters ounces as against the quarter ounce it would have weighed if folded into an ordinary envelope and sent without the protecting cardboard.

Air Force, have you ever heard an old adage that goes "Waste not, want not"?

September 8, 1971

MUCH OF OUR present woe of overproduction, overbuying and waste can be blamed on Madison Avenue (Manhattan), the ad boys' spiritual center.

Some readers may remember the classic bad-taste ad of all time that appeared in newspapers many years ago. TV hadn't been on the market very long and the ad men were pushing it. The ad in question, as we remember it, was a full-page one. It came out just before Christmas and it depicted a small girl hugging a rag doll, perhaps the most appealing pose of childhood. The child's eyes were filled with tears.

The actual words of the caption we can't recall. The gist was that the little girl's parents were causing her suffering by not buying a TV set. All the other little girls' and boys' parents in the neighborhood had one and she was being made fun of. Worse, she was shunned. The ad's intent was of course that parents be shamed into buying a set for a family Christmas present, so their child could again become a member of the human race.

No less a person than Eleanor Roosevelt protested publicly and the ad was withdrawn.

But in more subtle ways we are urged every day through our advertising media to buy, buy, BUY. Much of what we buy we don't need. We have too much already and we waste too much. We add to a growing pile of refuse which we find increasingly hard to dispose of. And our overbuying stuffs an ad man's pocket so he too can overbuy.

The Environmental Protection Administration says, "Unless we can stop fanatically producing and consuming more than we need, we won't have a world to stand on." Our young people seem to be showing us how we can get along in a simpler life, and be more contented in that life than we are now.

Is it possible for us who are older? We wonder.

September 29, 1971

SOME PEOPLE LOVE a constant noise, especially of radios, going all day long. Others don't. It is perhaps a little easier to give up noise than to be a prisoner of it — to have to listen to it when it is distracting or disturbing you.

Try to control noise pollution. Keep your car and motorcycle mufflers and tailpipes repaired. Blow your horn only in an emergency. Try not to play loud music or use power tools where their noises will disturb others.

If you are plagued by an industrial noise, such as power compressors, ask the offending industry to look into low-noise equipment. (There is a new power drill, for instance, that does not use compressed air.)

Remember, it is not known yet—although it is being studied—what noise is doing to our environment and ears. Are they being damaged beyond repair?

October 13, 1971

DID YOU KNOW that your poor john is now condemned as a polluter? "There are two crimes against humanity," says Dr. Donaldson Koons, chairman of Maine's Environmental Improvement Commission, "which at their inception seemed like real boons. They are the internal combustion engine and the flush toilet [which] create serious problems for our lakes and waterways." (And, he might have included, our air.)

Flush toilets contaminate vast amounts of water which are then released, polluting once-pure streams, lakes, and even the oceans. Dr. Koons recommends outhouses for summer camps as "the best disposal you can find." Martin Lang, New York City's Commissioner of Water Resources, agrees on the wastefulness of the flush toilet.

October 25, 1971

"THE BILLBOARD lobby never gives up," starts a recent editorial in the *New York Times*, which goes on to say that Congress, after passing a law in 1965 to restrict the number of billboards in the country, has finally gotten around to appropriating money (our tax money) to pay billboard owners for signs that under the law are to be removed. This, in spite of the fact that billboard owners, says the *Times*, are not owed anything since they exploit a road created by the public's funds.

A highway bill now pending in a House-Senate conference establishes a two-year moratorium on the removal of such billboards as give directional information (most do). "There is not the slightest reason," says the

Times, "for a two-year delay in a program already years behind."

Worse, a provision in the bill would permit six signs per mile on alternate sides of the road. "Instead of getting rid of the 800,000 billboards due to come down, this "tricky device" would allow them to stay. What's more, if they're properly spaced, another 400,000 would be permitted by the provision to be erected.

February 9, 1972

SINCE ONLY THREE hundred years ago, 359 animal species have become extinct. Now 800 more are on their way out. Up to the turn of the century even the dodo and the great auk existed. Then they disappeared. All we are ever going to see of these extinct animals are photographs, carvings, or those stuffed or of papier mache in natural history museums.

But not only animals are threatened by what we call progress. Of the 20,000 plant species in the world, one in ten, or 2,000, are becoming extinct, mostly because of urban and industrial spread.

We need our plants. Nearly all our crops and fruits have been developed from wild plants. Plants are necessary in nature's manufacture of oxygen; some of them as food for grazing animals; and many of them for our medicines.

It would be good if industries and developers transplanted carefully the plants that ordinarily are destroyed by bulldozers. But this is something that would have to be legislated, a long and arduous process. Rare is the builder who would do it voluntarily—the transplanting of plants takes time, and time is money.

March 15, 1972

REPORTS FROM Boston tell us that as of July 1, 1972, snowmobiles with a sound level of more than 82 decibels will be outlawed. After July 1, 1974, the ceiling is to be reduced to 73 decibels.

It is known that manufacturers can produce a relatively quiet snowmobile (the noisy machine gives its driver a sense of power and is therefore more readily saleable). One manufacturer, at least—the Outboard Marine Corporation—has promised Massachusetts Governor Sargent that it will manufacture a snowmobile to meet the 73-decibel standard by the July 1974 date.

Maine has a long way to go in regulating the noisome snowmobile.

October 18, 1972

THE LAW OF ECOLOGY is that everything has to go somewhere. Nothing just disappears into thin air. It is recycled by nature eventually—even if it takes a million years. (The disintegration process can be stopped, though, by poisons that kill bacteria, released from certain kinds of trash by the very bacteria that are doing the disintegrating.) Trouble is, our consumption of things sold in glass or tin or steel has reached staggering proportions, and continues to mount. We alive today need have only stirrings of fear. But what about our children? Our children's children? Or don't we care?

The United States now creates four and one-third billion tons of solid waste a year. Cost of disposal is four and one-half billion dollars. Disposal means burying or burning trash in our dumps or throwing it into our waters. Not too much imagination is needed to envision a blanket of dumps from Maine to California or a bore tide of displaced water flooding the land.

November 15, 1972

LAST MONTH Salt Creek, a pretty little stream that ordinarily gurgles gently through fourteen growing suburbs west of Chicago, went on a rampage. Salt Creek erupted, overflowed its banks, flooded basements and shopping centers and rushed over the tops of cars stalled by the flash flood. When the stream returned to within its banks there was found to be $25 million dollars worth of damage.

Why did this happen?

Ask the city planners and they will say, "We knew it would. We had warned of it." And so they had. Close off natural absorption of rain and snow, they said, by covering acres of land with concrete, asphalt, and rooftops and the overflow of streams can no longer be contained. Even when a community provides enough storm drains and stream revetments, flood damage will take place unless the community matches its newly built-up areas with areas where the rain runoff can be held until flood threat recedes.

Perhaps York County does not yet have the worry that spreading cities do — it still has wide areas of natural vegetation to absorb rain — but (town planners please note) under the present rate of expansion today's village is tomorrow's town. And the city of the day after tomorrow.

"The mills of the gods grind slow, but they grind exceeding well." The god of conservation got a slow start with *his* mill but, if not grinding exceeding well as yet, has at last put on speed. Town and city governments, citizen cooperation, literature, schools, the media — all are contributing to stem the waste that has at last made us fear its consequences.

A readable paperback, *50 Simple Things You Can Do to Save the Earth,* (children's version, same title, except substitution of "Kids" for "You") yields considerable help in changing our wasteful habits, and incidentally saving us money. If the book can't be found in some of the smaller bookstores, Kennebunk Book Port and Bookland in Biddeford, Saco, Wells, and Sanford have it.

Save The Wild Orchid

June 30, 1971

A YOUNG COUPLE, Kevin and "Hughie" Thorsell, visiting Kevin's parents, the Reverend and Mrs. Ernest Thorsell, Kennebunk, saw two things that excited and disturbed them as they rounded the bend past Howard Johnson's on the east side of the Maine Turnpike last Friday evening and rolled toward the toll booth.

First, Hughie caught a glimpse of wild orchids; then Kevin noticed, beyond them, a small red marker which indicated that bulldozing was imminent.

"The orchids must be saved," he says. A biology teacher at Proctor

The wild orchid, genus "calapogon pulchellus"

Academy and a Conservation Commissioner in Andover, New Hampshire, he speaks authoritatively. Enthusiastic bird and flower lovers, Kevin and Hughie spend their free time roaming the woods and beaches with binoculars.

They got out of their car. Among the purple orchids, miniatures of the large variety found hereabouts only in florist shops, they saw wild rhododendrons, sphagnum moss ("interesting that it can hold so much water"), and sundew (drosera rotundifolia), an insect-eating plant that "eats" a bug about the size of a no see-em, a biting midge. (This last plant, growing in nitrogenless soil, gets its nutriment instead from insects.)

The wild orchid – genus name "calopogon pulchellus" – grows in Minnesota, Ontario, Quebec, Newfoundland and south to the United States. It blooms from June to August. It likes the wet, acid soil of bogs, peat meadows, and swamps. It has loose clusters of from two to ten delicate purple flowers and it grows from two to twenty inches high with a single leaf sheathing its stem at the base. Another wild orchid found was the rose pogonia (Pogonia ophioglossoides). (It has a fringed lip that hangs downward. Its flowers are single, instead of in groups, and it has a broad, sheathing leaf midway on the stem. It blooms from June to August, and it grows four to twenty inches high in Minnesota, western Ontario, Newfoundland, and south, locally, to Florida on the coastal plain. It too likes acid soil of wet meadows and stagnant bogs. Both flowers like sun.

The Thorsells were excited about their find. They were also disturbed. The land the flowers and plants grow on has been taken by eminent domain by the Maine Turnpike Authority, presumably for expansion of the Howard Johnson complex on both sides of the turnpike and it appears to be only a matter of time before the land will be bulldozed.

Kevin suggested that Sterling Dow III (Conservation Commission's Coordinator for the Maine Natural Resources Council) be contacted, as well as the York County Audubon Society and local garden clubs. But it won't do, he says, for just anybody to dig up the wild orchid to save it. It should be dug by a knowledgeable group or person, the soil it will be placed in should first be tested, and much of the soil it now grows in should go with it; in other words, its environment should be transplanted along with the plant.

It is most important that the greatest restraint be used in picking our orchids, say horticultural books.

"The orchid should be saved," he said again. "So many areas it grows in have been destroyed, and it is so rare."

In spite of pleas by horticulturists and flower lovers in general, the orchids were bulldozed. In 1990, after the Maine Turnpike Authority's decision to widen the 'Pike (from York to South Portland), a referendum petition was circulated against the action; the petition garnered a record number of signatures, assuring the referendum's placement on the ballot. On November 5, 1991, the project was defeated 59% to 41%.

The transportation poll will require future examination of environmental consideration of flora, fauna, wetlands, etc.

Maine Yankee

July 15, 1972

IN WISCASSET, Maine, the nuclear age has finally caught up with Women's Lib—women are now allowed to go through the "Maine Yankee" nuclear reactor plant if they wear slacks—but it hasn't quite made it yet with Teens' Lib.

The plant is still in the charge of the contractor, whose insurance regulations permit no youngsters inside the buildings. Knowing this, a hundred or so Kennebunk High School students recently went up by bus just the same with science teacher William Cook for a briefing, given in a reception building at some remove from the plant itself. Too bad, said Al Packard of Kennebunk, one of the chaperones, "They're an awfully well behaved bunch of kids." Age has a few compensations: While the students ate their sandwiches, some of the chaperones, a couple reporters and one or two guests, hard hats atop their heads, were conducted on an hour's tour of the plant.

Before this, "Maine Yankee" information officers George Pillsbury and Donald Laubenstein talked to the students, answered questions and showed a movie of a similar plant in Connecticut. Part of their aim was to reassure doubters about the safety, to people and environment, of the $200 million complex of steel buildings ("the most expensive thing ever built in Maine, and all with private capital"), with its reactor containment dome that has the innocent look of a giant observatory. It could be inferred from what the speakers said that the reactor has all the danger potential of a kitten.

Why, then, the nagging little doubts?

First, radioactivity.

Nothing to it, says Mr. Laubenstein. With all the system's built-in safety devices—more in this plant than in either Russia's or England's or perhaps in all other atom-splitting operations throughout the world—the likelihood of radioactive material escaping is almost nil. The walls of the dome housing the reactor, that thing that splits the atom, are four-and-a-half-feet thick and if radioactivity should escape (unlikely, remember) it would be kept contained within the dome. At one point Laubenstein gestures to a white house about half a mile distant on a hill outside the steel mesh fencing that encloses the site. "Suppose the people in that house were to get five units of radioactivity from this plant. Normally to get that they would have to sit naked in the sun all day every day for a year. You'd get as much as five units just flying to California. From a wristwatch with a radium dial you get ten units. One chest x-ray a year means at least a hundred or two hundred units."

On to the next small nagging doubt. All that hot water flowing into the ocean at Wiscasset—will it raise havoc with our eco-balance?

About a quarter-mile from the complex of steel buildings, but still within the 790-acre site, sits an anachronism. A small wood house (once it must have been a farmhouse) is headquarters for environmental studies, started three years before plant construction commenced, to determine the effect of the reactor on its surrounding life. The studies will continue indefinitely, piling up records that will be compared with those to be assembled after plant operations begin. One of the creatures under study is the worm. No longer can that word be used to denote inferiority; this million-dollar commercial Maine crop has become important to the studies of marine life off the Wiscasset shores because the worm is probably the most temperature-sensitive creature of this particular environment. "The upper limit temperature tolerance of worms is about 80 degrees. We must be sure that at no time beyond our immediate discharge area does our temperature exceed that." It follows that the margin of safety for the sensitive worm shows at least as wide a margin of safety for other marine animals.

Laubenstein believes that the reactor will not harm marine life. "As soon as the water reaches open air it loses some of its heat," and, besides, Federal standards have been set up that permit in the mixing area (where the emerging hot water from the plant mixes with the Bay's cold water) only a one and a half degree elevation in summer's waters and four degrees in winter's.

Furthermore, the hot water is released under rigidly controlled conditions. Radioactivity builds up as the fissioning process (splitting of the atom) takes place. Periodically, X numbers of gallons of the radioactive water are drawn out and run through a purification plant. This removes 99.99% of all radioactive material. The low-level radioactivity left is then mixed with a huge volume of condenser-cooling water before it is discharged into the environment. "If this water weren't salt, it would meet public standards for drinking water. That's how clean it is." In effect, the plant will be discharging cleaner water than it will be taking in.

Well, what about the radioactive waste? Where can we get rid of it?

First, what causes the waste? In the beginning the spent fuel has high levels of radioactivity. Some of it decays away in seconds, some lasts hours, days, weeks, months, years, centuries. The spent fuel is stored at the station under water for sixty to ninety days while the short-term radioactivity decays. Then it is loaded into steel and lead cases for its journey to reprocessing centers by rail or truck (no plan to send it by water) so it can be used again. Radioactive material left after this is stored underground in steel tanks and will be kept under constant surveillance until all radioactivity decays away. And that, as someone has said, "will be some long time."

The Atomic Energy Commission is looking for more permanent ways of storing waste than in the present sludge-like pits. They are looking, for instance, at abandoned salt mines because the mines are dry, so chances of the stuff getting into water supplies are remote. But the AEC's study of this type of waste disposal in Kansas is meeting with opposition from that state. Undaunted, they are looking too at their Chairman Schlesinger's idea of shooting the waste into outerspace.

In spite of all the reassurances presented, perhaps the most comforting information to come out of the tour was this: On its way (and Russia is on the verge of a breakthrough) is fusion. Fusion is the combining—rather than the splitting, as in fission—of atoms to produce the same result: power. Fusion has no waste. Experts think the controlled fusion power plant will be practicable within twenty years.

In spite of the hard row the nuclear fission plants are having to hoe (i.e., an often fearful, inadequately informed public; antagonism from established fossil fuel plants; problems of waste disposal; etc.) the hard truth is that we are running out of fossil fuel. Unless we get power from some other source, our world will groan to a grinding stop.

And until something better comes along (the sun?—the tides?) that power will have to be furnished by nuclear fission.

Beyond a few correctable mishaps since its installation in 1972, Wiscasset's nuclear-powered Maine Yankee has escaped the fate of Three-Mile Island and Russia's Chernobyl. Since all is serene with Maine Yankee, according to its Energy Information Center, citizens' anxiety can smolder if not completely be laid to rest. There still remains the world's problem that won't go away: Where store all that mounting waste?

The Lost Town of Elms

October 11, 1972

ON MAIN STREET the tourist drew up to the curb and thrust an AAA trip-tych out the window. "Where's this town?"

I looked at where he was pointing. "I have no idea," I had to say. "Never heard of it. It must be a misprint."

It was not a misprint. At home I took out my map of Maine and there it was, the town of Elms, located about half way between Moody and Kennebunk. "Where is Elms?" I asked friends, neighbors—everyone. "Probably a town once," Portland's AAA said, "somehow kept on the maps when the town was gone."

Sentinels for the lost town of Elms / Photo by the author, 1972

Or lost, I am thinking now. Whether people still live there I do not know, nor do I want to know. Once I heard the sound of children's laughter—yes, I've been there, or nearly there, several times now—but the laughter was far away and when I heard it I turned and left. (Anyway, after yesterday I'm not going back any more.)

I stumbled on it this way: I stopped my car at a cemetery on Route One to give my dog a run. She played hide-and-seek among the tombstones—dogs have no respect for the dead—and then suddenly disappeared into woods at the far end of the cemetery. I headed for the spot where I had last seen her and soon she came racing toward me and half turned, as if to say, "Follow me."

On our way deeper into the cemetery the sounds of Route One had grown fainter, and now in the woods there was complete silence. Complete? There is no complete silence; there is only silence compared to noise—less noise, least noise. Out of the silence in the woods sounds began to emerge. Bird calls, solos that were sweet and intermittent with long pauses between trills . . . The sh-h-h sound a breeze makes when it lifts a million leaves and lets them fall again. Crickets. An army of them probably. So many that their continuous chirp became a silence in my ears. There were no other sounds. I could have been a hundred miles into deep forest.

At length the woods gave out onto a field. Here was evidence of man—a pile of cordwood, some logs. Otherwise the field was as God, or someone, had made it. A small blue wildflower—I don't know its name; we used to call it wild larkspur—grew in wandering patches. And here and there a maple or pine tree had sprouted a few inches, its seed doubtless dropped by a bird.

So noiseless was I in my sneakers that I nearly killed a chipmunk. I saw him suddenly, a hair away from my descending foot. Frozen by fear, his tiny body pulsated with his heart's hammering. My dog and I watched him until, as if released like a wound-up toy, he sped away, his route marked by the parting of the blue wildflowers.

A few yards farther on, a garter snake lay sunning in the path. Again I looked down just in time. The small corkscrew body was as still as the chipmunk's had been. Then with lightning speed it slithered off into the grass.

These were the only signs of life. Living life, that is. There were the evidences that man had been here—the cleared field, the cordwood, the logs, the path—and later on a scattering of granite posts, as if a miniature Stonehenge had been planned by someone and abandoned.

Woods began again abruptly at the far edge of the field and again there was a path. Not so well trodden, though, and leading through underbush, whereas in the first woods the bare-trunked pines sprang clean from a carpet of pine needles. These woods were, if possible, more quiet, this path more tortuous. There was a feeling of something waiting around each bend.

The path ended abruptly at a curve of road. Across the road, half hidden by trees, was a house of weathered shingles. On my left, another. There was no movement anywhere. I waited a few minutes. My dog had finished with darting on and off the path and stayed at my side. When I turned to go she kept close to me. We went back the way we had come—there seemed no other way—through the woods, across the field, through woods again, past the tombstones and out to my car. For an hour I drove the streets that bordered the cemetery. None led to the one I had just left.

As I said, I have made several visits to my lost town of Elms. I never break out of the woods, though, at the place of the bend in the road. When I begin to glimpse the houses through the trees, I turn back. Why? Am I afraid of the unknown? Afraid I would come upon a Shangri-La or an Islandia? A Brigadoon? No. My feeling is dread. Dread that the curve of the road will take me back to Route One, to gas stations, motels, and billboards—back, in fact, to Now.

I like the idea of a lost town, a town given life only by fantasy. I have peopled Elms. I have put barns behind its houses and in the barns I stabled horses and cows. Their manure is sweet in the October air and the cows are milked at eventide. I have put oil lamps on round wood tables in its kitchens, benches in front of its fireplaces. I have given the town a one-room schoolhouse. That's large enough for a town the size of Elms; no one there anyway needs to learn about computers or overpopulation or crime-in-the-streets. There is an old swimming hole in the river that winds through Elms and once I distinctly heard the laughter of young people on a load of hay as it rounded the bend.

I hear it still, even though the last time I was there (it was yesterday and I won't go again) another sound broke in. Faint at first, it grew louder until the bulldozer drowned out the sound of laughter.

Poor, foolish people of Elms. Did you think it would not find you?

I have strong feelings about the way life is here [in Maine]. You see I was raised here, way off in the country, so far we didn't have [near] neighbors. It was the kind of place where people and life were good. Then, one day, the bulldozers came and cut a strip through the middle of our county, dividing my world into sections. Then the strangers came, buying up everything . . . driving up the price of land and taxes. I've seen the place where I grew up divided and developed and destroyed so that it no longer exists, except in my memory.

You see, I went back home a few years ago and found a fence and a "no trespassing" sign around the place where I spent most of my growing-up life. I can't go there any more.

New Jersey was once beautiful as Maine. And so were New York and Massachusetts. Why do you think all those people come up here to Maine? They come here to see what their place looked like before they ruined it.

Richard Peek, a truck driver from Razorville, Maine, wrote the above essay which appeared in the November 1990 issue of *Maine Environment* and was recently broadcast in longer form on Public Radio's *Maine Things Considered*.

8

Potpourri

(Star, 12/21/61, News of the Past Dept., 75 years ago - "Some action must be taken by the executive council at no distant date on the case of Mrs. Barrows, the Kittery murderess, as her reprieve only extends to April when she must be hanged if nothing is done.")

The Case Of The Kittery Murderess

December 21, 1961

Dear "News of the Past"

Was action taken at no distant date
On that woman in Kittery who caused to vacate
A mysterious victim (was he loathsome, degenerate?
Chronic absintheate?
Or merely, to her, annoyingly celibate?)?
And how did she do it, this woman intemperate?
Did she fatally osculate?
Asphyxiate?
Aerate?
Or tend to his cold with arsenic chalybeate?
Don't leave me in this state.
Inform me, elucidate.
What was the fate of this killer inveterate?
Did the council, in April, la Barrows' life terminate?
Or let her continue, in peace, to extravagate?

Betty Joyce

Beryl Oswell, *Star* secretary, has done a bit of research on the murder case mentioned in the "News 75 Years Ago" column in the *Star* and in Betty Joyce's poetically humorous letter to the editor four or five weeks ago. This week Mrs. Oswell received the following letter from the *Portsmouth Herald*:

Dear Mrs. Oswell:

We are glad to be able to accommodate you in the matter of the Barrow's murder case. The feature story we carried on Dec. 22, 1958, ran at least three galleys long and obviously can't be covered in the brief space of a letter.

However, the state did charge and prove that Oscar Blaney and Mrs. Mary E. Cate Barrows did conspire to murder the woman's husband, Thomas Barrows. It was crudely done and fooled the police for only a day or two. They were tried and convicted. The court sentenced them to life in Thomaston.

Blaney, rebuffed in attempts to win parole, finally took the quick way out on Sept. 18, 1895, hanging himself in his cell. The woman was made of sterner stuff, as they often are, and to the end of her days fought stubbornly to get out from behind the walls. Her death, on Nov. 16, 1916, came almost 33 years to the day after the crime, and when she died, Mrs. Barrows was the lifer with the longest time in the penitentiary.

I hope this quick capsule of the Barrows' murder will be of service to you.

Very truly yours,
The Portsmouth Herald
Raymond A. Brighton
Managing Editor

Camelot/Kennebunkport Playhouse

July 16, 1965

THERE IS A castle in our midst. It sprang up Monday night and will vanish on Sunday. It belongs to King Arthur and its location is Camelot.

A newspaper reporter should stick to facts. We tried hard to. But for a magic two hours Monday night we were not in the fifth row of the Kennebunkport Playhouse. We were in Loewe and Lerner's "Camelot," where "winter cannot come until December . . . and the morning fog must disappear," where King Arthur, in the forest outside his castle, first meets the blonde Guinevere (Jenny) who has been sent to wed him, and where years later she and the pure knight Lancelot, to their dismay, fall in love.

King Arthur wasn't the smartest man in the world—or thought he wasn't. He had been only a page who'd been ordered back to his master's castle from London—where a jousting of knights was to take place—to fetch his master's sword. Leaving London, he saw a sword stuck in stone. "It'll save me the trip," he said to himself, and proceeded to pull Excalibur from the rock. This, if you remember legend, makes him King of England.

Helping him train for his kingly duties is magician Merlin who prepares him for every contingency but one. "Why haven't you taught me love and marriage?" cries Arthur, just before Guinevere is due to arrive.

"Don't scramble them together that way. They are two different things," Merlin replies, evading the question.

Merlin lives backward. He doesn't age, he's static, and he eases out of the play early on. His powers are diminishing. "I have lost my memory of the future," he says as he moves off-stage and out of Arthur's life.

Arthur and Jenny live happily for several years, until Arthur's plan of a Round Table (seating only the purist of knights, who will work for peace) brings a French knight galloping to the castle to join up. Lancelot is *so* pure, Jenny scorns him. "When I see you going by on your horse," she tells him just before a jousting tournament, "I shall be thinking 'there he goes, there he goes—the sermon on the mount.'"

Inevitably love springs up between them. Even so, the situation might be saved but for Modred. Modred is a sneaky one, out to wrest Arthur's kingdom from him and turn the knights into medieval delinquents. He admits even his own father hates him: "Mother had a youth potion that took off ten years. When I was nine, father gave it to me — to make me minus one."

And Jenny: "There is one thing I can say for Modred. He is bound to marry well. *Everybody* is above him."

Camelot does not have the traditional happy ending, but you will thrill to Igor Gavon's Arthur, dredging up out of his life's wreckage a beam of hope. And you may weep a little for those star-struck lovers, Judith Hastings' Guinevere and Jay Stuart's Lancelot. Even if you don't weep, you'll be struck by their beauty. (Jenny's profile against a black curtain drop is something to remember.) You'll hate Louis Ibarrondo's Modred, as you should, and you will roar at R. E. Sinclair's Pellinore, appearing first on stage with a huge, mangy-looking sheep dog that did not want to leave the stage on opening night (the ham).

Be sure not to miss this rollicking, carolling, lusty, colorfully costumed and staged musical. The boards of our barn playhouse have rarely resounded with such song and frolic, and its rafters have seldom looked down on more accomplished performances by more attractive players.

The decision - on which of the two outstanding theaters of the south Maine coast to be represented in this chapter - was a hard one. The Kennebunkport Playhouse and, twelve miles south, the Ogunquit Theater (hereafter referred to as Playhouse and Theater), rained top quality entertainment for decades on natives and vacationers during the summer. A choice of the two had to be made by the publisher. It was beyond me (who had attended opening nights as critic for the *Star*). I'm not sure, incidently, that Robert (Bob) Currier, owner and entrepreneur of the Playhouse, or John Lane, ditto of the Theater, were overjoyed at my moving as a critic, inexperienced and therefore unqualified, into their domain.

They need not have qualms. The two men for the most part selected unerringly, for a barn in Kennebunkport or the elegance of a built-for-theater building in Ogunquit, what the summer public would enjoy. The publisher chose *Camelot*. Both theaters had presented *Camelot*, only with different casts and at different times, and both were successful.

But the Playhouse is no more and the publisher's choice, then, becomes a kind of memorial. The barn died by fire; it was the second attempt on its life by flames. Official records must exist but my information stems mainly from James Burroughs, Fire Administrator for Kennebunkport: "The first fire was in 1947. There had been a theft at the Booth Tarkington estate at the same time that same night. It was probably started to distract attention from what was going on at the Tarkington place." Consensus of the villagers was - "strangers." No local person, they argued, would have vandalized so revered an institution as the Playhouse. The barn was restored and continued as before until finally ("sometime in the seventies") it burned to the ground. It is not known how this fire started, perhaps this time it was not by strangers but by some local misfit or mischievous child. We seem anyway not so scandalized by vandalism as we once were.

So I think of this update as a kind of memorial for Bob Currier, who for decades kept alive the concept of drama-in-the-barn, opening the door for small towns into other worlds and other personalities than their own. And a memorial too for the Playhouse, one of the last of its breed.

An old barn.

The New Math

October 27, 1965

"THE NEW MATH." Words to strike terror into the hearts of adults, especially parents. Because, let's face it, who wants our young ones to know more than we do, especially when the young ones are so young (kindergarten is when they start on this)? How are you going to like it when your toddler comes to you and says "Please Mommy (or Daddy), does this arithmetic relationship have the symmetrical property or the transitive?" And you're going to have to say, "Huh?"

Cheer up. Just be glad you're not a teacher. On the other hand, you might wish you were taking the stimulating course in the New Math for Kennebunk and 'Port grade school teachers this fall at the Park Street School. We drifted over ourselves last Thursday and joined the buzzing throng in the gymnasium that sat at long tables with books on the New Math in front of them. An attractive, white-haired woman busied herself in the foreground with an overhead projector. Behind her was the screen, suspended in midair. At one minute to four, the chatter died down and the woman started to speak. Except for a ten-minute coffee break, Mrs. Wilma Rollins of Nasson College and the University of Maine talked for two hours on her subject.

We ourselves have mastered the multiplication tables and can add and divide after a fashion, but algebra has always had the sound of a disease to us. Geometry means just something that in another form applies to a type of modern paintings. Logarithms? What's that? Nevertheless, at the end of a class that had already met several times and was well beyond the introductory stages, we found ourselves with at least a snubbing acquaintance with one aspect of the New Math: the three properties "reflexive, symmetrical and transitive." Just don't ask us to explain them.

If confronted with the New Math, don't feel stupid. The teachers themselves are having a struggle. At times during the two-hour lecture sighs and groans formed a kind of Greek chorus to questions from the floor that revealed a profound bewilderment. But, "She's certainly a marvelous teacher," said a young woman sitting next to us. "If anyone can get it across, she can."

Basically, the New Math is the theory of sets. (Isn't the idea of two sets, for example — one with one object in it and the other with two objects — simpler than the abstract numerals 1 and 2?) Once, to illustrate the partitioning of a set, Mrs. Rollins divided the teachers into eye-color groups. "All the blue-eyed people stand over there. Now all the brown eyes go into that corner. Any green eyes here? You stand in that corner. How about hazel? All the hazel people over there." (There was one grey-eyed person. Five sets in all.)

"Please notice something now," said Mrs. Rollins. "Three things. There is nobody sitting at the tables. This relation ('has the same color eyes as') has partitioned everybody in the original set into five different subsets. And nobody belongs to two groups. Suppose I took the relation 'is the same age as' — now these groups would all be split up differently. Nobody would be sitting down, and everybody would belong to at least one of these groups, and nobody would belong to more than one. Thank you very much, ladies and gentlemen. You may sit down."

Later, she discussed number. "We have talked about numbers but we have not talked about *number* at all. The idea of number is a completely abstract idea. Nobody ever sees a number. You can see a tree, but when I just say the word "tree" you do not see tree. It is a name we made up to apply to a thing that has the qualities of a tree. Primitive people could answer the question 'How many things do you have?' only by saying 'as many as something else.' They could match up. 'Do you have as many dogs as that fellow? We'll take them out and match them up.'"

She discussed "equivalents" (two sets are matched, or are equivalent, if they can be placed in one-to-one correspondence): "I had a daughter," she said parenthetically, "who taught first grade in California. Her pupils loved the word 'equivalent.' Children love big words. Why give them baby words like 'matched' when they love 'equivalent?'"

One of the things the New Math tries not to do is to tell children something that may have to be retracted later. Don't say you can't take 7 away from 4, because later on there is a 'negative 3'. Say, "We don't know any number now but later you will."

The whole idea behind the drastic change in the teaching of mathematics is this: The old way was a mechanical process. This new way enables children to see the reasoning behind what they are doing. "For example," said Mrs. Rollins, when we spoke with her after the session, "how would you multiply 32 by 19?"

We wrote it down:

$$\begin{array}{r} 32 \\ \times\quad 19 \\ \hline 288 \\ 32 \\ \hline 608 \end{array}$$

"Why did you indent 32?" she asked us.

"We have no idea."

"That's what I mean. You don't know WHY you did it that way. What you're really doing is this:

$$\begin{array}{rr} 30 \text{ plus} & 2 \\ 10 \text{ plus} & 9 \\ \hline & 18 \\ & 20 \\ & 270 \\ & 300 \\ \hline & 608 \end{array}$$

You are multiplying 2 × 9, 2 × 10, 30 × 9, 30 × 10. Children soak up the New Math so much easier than we can," she added, "because they have nothing to unlearn—and we have so much!"

School Superintendent John Seekins, writing about the New Math in our 1964 Town Report, said that the Kennebunk schools were front-runners with modern mathematics at the junior high and high school levels. They believe in modern mathematics for all grades, and they have effective programs in grades 7 through 12, but they have been cautious about introducing it into the elementary grades. For grades 1 through 6 they haven't found a modern mathematics textbook or a program that provides a balance between the new philosophy and the need for drill in the fundamental processes.

In the meantime the teachers are learning about it, so when the proper textbook appears they will be all set to march into the classroom, face a sea of small faces, and begin, "Now as to the reflexive property . . . "

Terror has lessened somewhat since the new math came to be considered a mutation, according to Maine School Administrative District 71

Superintendent Leo Martin. "New math concepts were excellent," he says, "but they were thrown onto the public so suddenly that not everybody understood it." Turns out the conceptions are not new after all but can be traced to the beginning of the century when a form of what was later called "the new math" was in general use by scientists and mathematicians. It is more than twenty years since that initial setback caused parents to throw up their hands at the intricacies of what their fledglings were having to learn – although kids for the most part absorbed the new thinking process quicker than did adults, entrenched as we were in the *old* math. The space program prodded general acceptance of the new math ("It began right after the Russians launched Sputnik in 1957," Amos McCallum, Chairman of the Mathematics Department at Kennebunk High School, told us) because much of it honed the thinking of the scientists and mathematicians who were working diligently to get us into outer space.

The Lafayette Elm Has Surgery

February 5, 1969

IT WAS A GREY morning last week when a KLPD (Kennebunk Light and Power District) truck drew up to a large elm on Storer Street. Three men got out and approached the tree. They walked around it for a few moments, looking up into its branches. Then one got back into the truck and drove it onto the lawn. Another climbed into the truck's cherry picker which the driver raised and swung over to one of the cables that hold the weight of the massive limbs. Thus began the severing of the Lafayette Elm's largest limb.

The branches were cut first, branches that in winter had laid their black tracery on winter snow for as long as the oldest resident can remember, and in summer had bounced neighborhood children and swept the green-

The demise of The Lafayette Elm / Photo by the author, 1969

sward beneath. Foot by foot the cutting crept toward the crotch where limb joined trunk.

The Leech Nursing Home borders one side of the acre of land the tree's spread covers. On the opposite side is the Storer Mansion where the Marquis de Lafayette — that same Lafayette who had served in the colonists' armed forces during our Revolution — was invited for tea when he visited Kennebunk in 1825.

In 1982, on the site of the old Lafayette elm, and after all attempts to save it had failed, another elm — this time the disease-resistant Groenveldt — was planted with appropriate ceremony in what is now called Lafayette Park. The next year a Maine-quarried boulder, soon to bear a plaque, was placed as companion to the new elm. In addition to a brief history of the ancient elm, the plaque bears the names "Town of Kennebunk" and "James P. Storer."

Storer is a lineal descendant of Colonel Joseph A. Storer who had built the mansion (it is still there) bordering the east side of Lafayette Park. In it Colonel Storer and his wife had hosted the Marquis de Lafayette on his return visit in 1825 to the country where he and his troops had helped turn the tide of the Revolution in the colonists' favor.

Although it is a widely-shared belief that the general had stood under the elm during his visit to review troops, there appears to be no factual basis for this. He must, though, have looked out from the Storer mansion and seen the young tree that was later to bear his name and to become the official symbol of the Town of Kennebunk.

A Look Back In Time

December, 1969

FROM TIME TO time we run across an old issue of the *Eastern Star,* predecessor of the late *Kennebunk Star* and the *York County Coast Star,* We'd like to share with you what is in it, to remind us that life was very different not so very long ago.

An April 19, 1918, issue discovered by Caroline Wallace of Kennebunk recently while she was cleaning out her attic yields some quaint items — not the least of which was the fact that the paper sold for "$1.00 a year, in Advance."

Advertisements covered a third of the front page, the biggest being those of Bonser & Son, clothiers, and NET & T Co. Smaller advertisers were George E. Cousens who sold seeds and asked customers to "call any-time after sunrise"; W.F. Brian, a painter and decorator ("1918 new advance patterns in wallpapers, French & English have just arrived"); and A.W. Meserve, an apothecary.

There were insurance company balance sheets, a notice that Hope Cemetery was raising its lot-care charge to $2 per year, and digging and filling (!) graves to $3.50 "as a result of the increased cost of labor and materials" (sound familiar?), and under the heading "Lost!" a black and gray striped shawl (anybody wear shawls today?). Dr. W.T. Cox, osteopath, wanted people to know that he graduated under the founder of the science; and W.C. Bigelow, civil engineer, that he was also an architect and land surveyor.

News was that over 3 percent of Kennebunk's total population, which was then 3,099, was now enlisted (World War I), and Judge Harold H. Bourne, town historian, had been appointed to keep a record of local enlistments "that none may be overlooked when the history is written." Maine had to furnish 222 men that year. Those subject to call from the area now covered by the *Star* were Chester E. Hilton, Ogunquit; Arthur Turgeon, North K'port; Ralph O. Evans, Kennebunk; and Ralph E. Perkins, Cape Neddick.

An *Eastern Star* was returned to the office with an unsigned letter: "Found in a sleeping car in Youngstown, Ohio. The Eastern Star is a long way from home, but your editorial, *The Key Man*, is worthy of most favorable comment. Keep up the good work." And under "Boy Scouts" was the announcement that because of the snow storm cooking tests were postponed until the next meeting. (Come on, boys — the girls would have made it.)

Under *News of 25 Years Ago*, a farmer claimed that "this (1893) is going to be a big grasshopper year, for the snow is going off without a rain storm. This is a sure sign, which the records of years past will prove." The log train was run on the Western division of the Boston & Maine Sunday for the first time that season. It came to Kennebunk after logs for the Portland Star Match Company.

Deacon Issacher Wells of K'port died Saturday, aged ninety-eight years, leaving a widow to whom he had been married sixty-three years, and seven of their twelve children . . . David Clark of K'port launched "a strong and finely modeled tug boat built for the New England Dredge Company of Boston." The boat was 128.34 tons, 96 feet length and 21 feet beam.

A house for sale advertised a lure that would entice few today — "small stable connected" . . . The Red Cross got $2,282.65 from its drive . . . Fire destroyed the Millner House . . . and the K'bunk road commissioner for eight years refused to accept reappointment if all he could have was $1,500 for his share of the road money.

On the second page, editorials were brief (five inches), bland, and strangely, had nothing to do with Kennebunk or even Maine. One discussed the anti-tipping bill in Massachusetts. "As originally drawn," went the editorial, "the bill provided that the receiving of gratuities for checking clothing should be prohibited, but it was changed so as to allow employees to receive 'tips' on the understanding that these must not be turned over to the employer. Governor McCall (Massachusetts) played safe by failing either to sign or veto the measure. Watch for the joker in this law."

The other, in its entirety: "Oregon ducks, as well as Oregon humans, must eat substitutes, by order of the food administration. Small potatoes, too small, in fact, for the farmer to have paid any attention to ordinarily, are said to have solved the problem, when mixed with carrots and other materials, minus wheat. No doubt the ducks are thriving on the new rations and quacking for more."

The annual mixed double tennis tournament, sanctioned by the U.S. Lawn Tennis Association, was scheduled for Arundel Casino, K'port, in August. Waterfront real estate was a steal: "Summer Cottage for Sale, 5,000 ft. of land, ocean view. Will sell for $1,200." And a fifteen-acre wood lot was $500. Both bore a name well known today in the Kennebunk area: Bowdoin.

Scattered throughout the paper are palliatives for what must have been the major physical complaints of the time: kidney and bladder problems and constipation. "Don't use harsh physics . . . Get Doan's Regulets. They operate easily . . . " Mrs. William Young, Fletcher Street, reported, "My kidneys act too frequently, and that is a great annoyance. Doan's Kidney Pills have helped me . . . " Who ever said our forebears were more reticent than their descendants?

Clothes were surprisingly expensive (but it was a war year), women's coats $15 to $50, suits $20 to $40, dresses $10 to $35, blouses $.98 to $10, and hats $3.98 to $10 at W.E. Youland Co. in Biddeford.

The last page of the four-page *Star* was devoted to an ad by Rogers Fibre Co. on The Third Liberty Loan: A sketch, if not by James Montgomery Flagg, then in his style, of men in trenches, bayonets at the ready, and a stretcher case borne by medics; and the words, "What about the boys who are fighting for you in France? For them, the trenches; the pitiless storms of rain and sleet; the ceaseless deafening bombardment of the guns; hunger, cold and fever; wounds and death. For you — a little economy and deprivation. Are you complaining because 'war time' means coal shortage; less sugar in your coffee; less money than you think you ought to make?"

We end with a little editorial of our own: The April 19, 1918, issue came out during World War I, the "war to end all wars" fought only fifty years ago. Since then we have been involved in three major conflicts, one "real," two undeclared. One thing about an undeclared war, it may be just like any other war . It may even be more expensive. But it sure doesn't deprive the folks back home of anything.

We vaguely remember in World War I the joy of our parents on discovering, in the corner of a remote shelf, a forgotten pound of sugar. More clearly, we recall the strict rationings of World War II. But it was business as usual in the Korean War; and in the Vietnam War, who lacks for staples, even luxuries . . . ?

No, an undeclared war doesn't deprive the folks back home of a thing. Except, of course, their sons.

Cushioning Future Shock

January 27, 1971

I AM NOT VERY inventive. In my lifetime I have had only three what you might call inventive ideas. The first grew out of irritation, the second desperation, and the third nostalgia.

Crawling on my stomach with a vacuum one day to get at the dirt under couch and tables and chairs, I thought, "Why not furniture suspended on chains from the ceiling? And tables that slide out of walls?" The idea stayed unborn in my mind as too radical. Now, of course, such furniture, although not accepted widely, has been on the market for some time, invented by someone else who I suppose is reaping sizeable profits.

And once years ago, after days of buffeting by the resentful ocean we were traveling on, I muttered, "I'm getting darned sick and tired of this." Instantly there flashed into my mind a gyroscopic room and I saw a queue lined up waiting its turn at the equilibrium the room supplied. Five minutes and they'd emerge ready to tackle the roll and pitch again.

This idea too was brought to fruition by someone else. Whom I don't know, but Chichester sailing around the world in his *Gypsy Moth* plotted the day's course in a gyroscopic chair.

My latest brain child is for those who, seeing an age pass, want to grab hold of its coattails and slow it down. It has to do with how working conditions are becoming well-nigh perfect. Look at the cubicles in our skyscraper office buildings—as slick as architects and decorators can make them. See those manicured landscapes surrounding the industrial complexes of steel and glass that line our highways.

In one such building the entire office force works in one enormous room whose walls and ceiling deaden sound, whose floors are carpeted wall to wall, whose delicately tinted walls are free of paintings or photographs. Tall and leafy plants abound in this room, and thrive; they would be fired if they didn't. A gleaming restaurant serves meals, but for those who want snacks an aluminum wagon makes the rounds with sandwiches and pastries in plastic bags and coffee from an electric urn.

The executive hierarchy, as one of them puts it, is determined by the height of the grillwork partitions surrounding their desks. Telephones in this room don't ring, they whisper. The typists and bookkeepers park their cars in an underground garage. The building has been created by sound experts, by time-and-motion experts, by visual experts for the workers' comfort and, it follows, their increased efficiency.

All this may not have the desired result.

Why rush the discords in, asks the poet, but that harmony might be prized? Too much harmony can bore. I visualize small fights that start and are kept perking to put some pizazz into the working day. Things that passed unnoticed in the hurly-burly of the old office become distractions against monochromatic walls and in the velvet quiet of sound proofing. A vivid skirt, a jazzy tie can pack the wow of an Andy Warhol poster. A slightly raised voice becomes a shout. I wager that efficiency will drop—perhaps is already dropping—that discontent will flourish and bewildered experts will install deeper carpets, trim the grass a little closer and add martinis to the snack wagon.

But I suggest that things stay the way they have become. Only install a small room somewhere in the building, a replica of the old-type office. It would contain no noiseless typewriters, no soft carpets. Its telephone would have the decibel count of a police siren. Its walls would bear pictures of the company's past presidents; the plant when it was only a story high; that well-remembered Christmas office party back in '36; and Mabel, the office file clerk and typist, at the baby shower the girls gave her. All of the photographs hang crooked.

The floor of this office is covered with linoleum, curling slightly where it has spread at the seams so everyone trips over it. The file drawers bear cards "A-C, D-G," etc.; the type is worn off by time and only memory can determine what is where. The manila folders inside are spongy with age—they date from when the company was founded—and the records they hold have been filed largely incorrectly. But Mabel had always known where to find them—opening the drawer, shutting her eyes briefly and unerringly pulling out what the boss asked for.

The desk, bearing a seashell ashtray stained from two decades of cigar butts and cigarettes ground out by ten thousand salesmen, has a snag on the left lower drawer. Someone was always going to repair it but never got around to it, and Mabel had a chronic run in her left stocking. Next to the desk, for salesmen to sit on, is an old dining room chair, fragile as a Louis XVth; the leather seat is split and the stuffing oozes out.

Windows are opaque from past rains and snows and soots. They are covered with chintz that Mabel once hung to give the office some zip. Limp now, glaze gone, colors faded, their ball fringe swings gently in today's air conditioning that was yesterday's draft. The radiator steams, and a discerning eye might see the ghosts of past office girls who hovered over it in mid-winter, warming cold hands and cold behinds. Atop one of the files is an electric plate, beside it a jar of instant coffee, Coffee-mate, a box of cube sugar, an empty cardboard container that once held chocolate doughnuts, and three mismatched cups with spoons in them. There used to be four coffee cups. The fourth now holds an ivy plant that is never watered. It receives moisture from the radiator in winter, from humidity in summer. It neither grows nor dies.

If my suggestion is acted on, this is a room whose door will be opened daily to admit one by one the employees of a modern office. The room will function as a retreat, much as a chapel does. No prayers will be uttered in it, no soul-searching undergone, but the girls will sit, in turn, where Mabel once sat. They will stretch forth their fingers and hear the satisfying clatter of an ancient L.C. Smith typewriter. The executive in charge of the Northwest Division, Southern Ohio and Kentucky, enters next and perches on a corner of the desk. "Take a letter, Mabel — I mean Sandra." He will grind out his cigarette in the ashtray that somehow still smells of the sea. Sandra: "How about a cup of coffee, Ted?" (She usually calls him Mr. Brophy.)

She puts the pot on and they work while it comes to a boil. Then they drink their coffee and relax and gossip awhile. Absolutely nothing "goes on" between them. They enjoy knowing that it could if they wanted it to — in privacy.

After a while Mr. Brophy gets up. "Well, back to the ribbon counter," he says. Sandra joins him. They go to the door, open it and leave, refreshed and ready to face the remainder of the day.

I give this idea to whoever wants it. I feel that if our great industrial network is to survive it must not only sometimes look backward, it must experience a slice of yesterday. The past has its charm, its balance. Let us take its message with us to cushion our future shock.

Maine Seals

Excerpted from a series of articles,
August 9 - September 15, 1971

ONE EVENING in June several years ago Mr. Peter Gunn, who lives near the bridge over the Mousam River on Route 9, was attracted to the river by a sort of commotion. He saw his dog Spot, a miniature shepherd, pulling by the scruff of the neck a baby seal up out of the water and onto the bank. Mr. Gunn helped him. After the baby was safely ashore the little shepherd licked him dry and then lay down on top of him in a comfortable shallow hole in the flower garden where both spent the night sound asleep.

The next morning Mr. Gunn tried to give the little seal water and then cod liver oil from a medicine dropper, but for some reason the baby was unable to swallow. Opening his mouth, Mr. Gunn pushed his finger down its throat, and, by pressing hard on a sort of membrane or lump that seemed to be there, broke it. After this the seal could swallow but even then did not eat a great deal. He weighed only about 25 pounds.

From the first the seal and the whole family were fast friends. When Mr. Gunn came home at night and called "Sealie, Sealie," the little seal would answer him by short barks and waddle toward him, and the family often took him riding in the car where he would crawl up behind the back seat and go to sleep.

As Sealie grew older Mr. Gunn got him to eat a little fish besides the cod liver oil, and gave him swimming lessons. For Sealie at first didn't know how to swim. When placed in the water he would sink. So Mr. Gunn held him up while the baby, almost like a real child, paddled around until finally he mastered his natural skill.

All this time Sealie and Spot, who had been quite a rover until Sealie's arrival, were the closest of friends. They slept together at night and the dog kept watch over Sealie by day, although sometimes Sealie waddled out onto Route 9 and Spot had to follow. Then motorists would stop and knock on Mrs. Gunn's door and say, "Missus, do you know you have a seal out on the road?"

*About three months after Sealie had first come to the Gunns, and had gotten to weigh about 50 pounds, he took off one evening down the river and was not seen for a week. Then one afternoon he reappeared, climbed the bank and spent the night with Spot as before. The next morning he coasted off toward the sea again. Soon after this a friend told Mr. Gunn that he had seen some men standing on the bridge shooting at a young seal on the mud by Mr. Gunn's house. None of the Gunns ever saw Sealie again.**

Seals. One of nature's most beguiling creatures. It may be their fur, soft and pliant as a puppy's. Or their eyes — soulful orbs that seem to say, "Please be kind. I trust you."

Controversy rages internationally over the arctic seal, clubbed to death for that soft fur that will reappear on women's backs (the unisex fad is placing it on men's backs as well). And now there is growing controversy over the one called "harbor seal" that ranges Maine coastal waters and whose numbers seem to be diminishing yearly. Is this apparent decrease due to shooting? They are shot, but whether this is causing them to vacate — if they are — Maine waters is debatable.

Mrs. Thomas Liversidge, who recently watched the shooting of seals from her window at Crescent Surf, Parsons Beach: "They were being shot at from a lobster boat. This wasn't the first time. A small seal was washed up early in July. We didn't realize it had been wounded until we tried to put it back in the water. It swam off. It wasn't completely dead but it came back on shore with the next wave. A Canadian man happened along. He asked if he could take it to a vet. He got it into his car and drove off." Shooting has been heard by others interviewed who live along the beaches but they have seen nothing of actual shooting — only an occasional seal washed up later on the shore.

Lobster fisherman rightly or wrongly are suspected of the shooting. Some have been heard to say a seal can eat a bushel of lobsters a day and shatter traps to get at the lobster bait inside. But the last survey on seals by the Maine Department of Sea and Shore Fisheries states: "Seal damage to lobsters is practically non-existent . . . there was a herd of seals (in the Skillings River) thought to be feeding on soft-shelled lobsters. A check . . . showed that they did not remain in the river to feed but went

*By Elizabeth D. McMaster, reprinted by permission from the author.

out into the bay where herring and squid were plentiful. A large seal showed nothing in its stomach but squid beaks. It is reported by lobstermen that seals sometimes follow their boats picking up items being thrown in the water, including short lobsters. They probably do pick them up, but whether with their soft mouths and throats they are capable of chewing and swallowing them is doubtful."

Harry Goodridge of Rockport, Maine, somewhat of an authority on seals, reported that a laboratory in Salisbury Cove had three seals they were using in a kidney experiment. One day, when the seals were starving because they were mistakenly underfed, "I was near a lobster pound, could have all the lobsters I wanted. I'd throw in raw lobsters. The seals would go for them, but then they'd leave them alone. Then I tried raw lobster meat. Then cooked. Soft shells. Hard shells. They just would not eat a lobster. I'd throw in a sculpin and they'd gulp it down."

Shooting now is allowed for the most part. Protection of seals is sparse. The only Maine law prohibiting shooting (Private and Special Laws Relating to Sea and Shore Fisheries) states:

No person shall during months of June, July and August destroy seals in Casco Bay and in the waters between Branch River in the Town of Kennebunk and the easterly end of Goose Rocks Beach in the Town of Kennebunkport, by shooting with rifle or other long-range weapon which might endanger human life under a penalty of $50 for each offense or by imprisonment of not more than thirty days.

Section II. Hunting seals near Green Island is forbidden. It shall be unlawful between May 15 and October 15 for any person to hunt, shoot at or kill any seal within two miles of any part of Green Island in Western Bay in the County of Hancock.

Sometime the middle of May, after nine and half months in its mother's womb, the (usually single) baby harbor seal is born. The mother had left the herd for the birthing and gone to one of a variety of places — a marsh, an island — her chief requirement that it be as far from man as possible.

Her newborn seal has all its faculties. It may or may not be born with a soft white fur, a disappearing adaptation to the birth's having taken place in former ages on ice floes. The fur — coveted by fur coat manufacturers — is gone the second day, occasionally is shed even before birth.

The baby nurses and sleeps away its first twenty-four hours and then is given its first plunge into water by its mother. It grows fast. At birth it weighs 20 pounds, is 34" long; at three months 60 pounds, 38"; at a year 90 pounds, 50". An adult female weighs 170 pounds, an adult male 130; the length of both is 60". An adult is capable of traveling 12-15 m.p.h. but cannot maintain this speed for more than a half hour.

The female trains her pup intelligently. Its first week of life is without fear of man, so the mother submerges it when a boat approaches. In the water the pup follows its mother as she forages for fish. Nursing cannot take place in water so the two return to the ledges for it. The little one, whose cry resembles that of a bleating lamb, is born without teeth, but they come fast—within a day or two—and nursing is supplemented by fish in three to five weeks. When the pup is weaned, in about six weeks toward the last of June, the mother guides it to where fish is plentiful and leaves it. The young seal then begins to mix with the herds. Up to this time the concern of the mother for the pup is manifold. An example of this was when the mother of a pup caught in a net was seen to hit the net repeatedly in rapid succession by jumping from the water and landing on it in an attempt to free her baby.

Mating is thought to take place during the second and third weeks of August when mature seals disappear from the herds. Later in August the mature animals rejoin the herd. Battered and scarred males are then seen recuperating in seclusion. Dr. B. Havinga in *Seals in Holland Waters* says he "was unable to observe fighting between the males and the breeding activity and so assumed that it took place in the water." It is thought seals move offshore to the more remote islands and ledges for their mating.

In summer, in the southern part of Maine, seals' daily activity is determined by two things: location of food and tides. During low tide the seals crawl onto the rocks and sun themselves, and because rocks are scarce in southern Maine they can be heard grunting and barking, trying to perch on what space there is.

In the more northern part of Maine, ledges are free of water at all stages of tide and the seals' activity is determined more by the fish it eats. If schooling fish are present the seals follow till they have had enough to eat or the school is scattered; then they crawl out to sun themselves and sleep. If there are no schooling fish the seals are inclined to scatter more and forage for groundfish and squid. Their varied diet includes tom cod, flounder, herring, pollack, octopus, etc. In other words, they eat mostly what they find.

In late October or November, after about a week of freezing weather, fish and other marine forms move offshore to somewhat warmer and deeper waters. Seals follow, occupying the outer islands and ledges which become their winter homes. They do not range far or long from them. Inshore movement starts sometime in April. The first to arrive are the pregnant females and the young of the preceding year.*

Harry Goodridge has trained seals for a number of years. It came about this way: Once he hunted a great deal—"No more. I got sick of the sight of blood" — and for his water kills used Chesapeake retrievers. They were good swimmers but, as it turned out, unable to keep up with scuba divers of which Harry Goodridge is one, who besides spending much of his time off the ground as a tree surgeon spends almost an equal amount underwater.

Why not, he thought, train a young seal to retrieve for him? A seal would be companionable too. Time spent underwater can be very lonely. So "I tried to find out about seals. I asked fishermen, where do seals have their babies? What time of year? Nobody could tell me anything."

Harry explored on his own, picking up a few young seals and bringing them back to an enclosure he had made and placed in the harbor for study and training purposes. Later, traveling to Florida to learn how porpoises were trained, he became friends with a trainer named Andre, and when Andre died, Harry named his favorite young seal after him.

Andre the seal is famous. He has been the subject of numerous magazine articles, including one in *Life*, and has been on TV—like another marine animal whom he holds in contempt. "What do you think of Flipper?" Harry asks Andre. Andre emits a healthy raspberry, Andre blows his nose on Harry's handkerchief. He blows his whistle. Dribbling a basketball down the pool, he noses it at us and through a hoop. He curves smoothly through a suspended tire—and then shows you how it was when he was learning, getting stuck halfway and lying draped over the tire in discouragement.

Harry kicks him, a pretend kick, and Andre grabs his trouser leg, releasing it only on utterance of the magic word "fish." Harry cocks a forefinger at Andre and says "Bang!" Andre rolls over dead. (At least once Andre has managed to upend with a piece of seaweed on his chest repos-

*Text of the above section based on *The Atlantic Harbor Seal Coastal Waters of Maine*, a survey made in 1947 by John H. Hunt and published in 1948 by Maine Department of Sea and Shore Fisheries.

The illustrious Andre of Rockport / Photo by the author, 1969

ing like a lily on the bosom of a corpse.)

One time Henry, deciding that Andre might be taught to carry mooring lines from the dock out to boats in the harbor, made a harness and started to put it on Andre. The seal fought it. And continued to fight until Henry threw down the harness and stalked off, without giving Andre his customary dinner of herring.

When Henry's temper cooled, he went back to the pool to try again. He didn't have to. Andre was wearing the harness. Andre had known right along what he was supposed to do. He just hadn't wanted to do it. But no harness, no herring. So he got into the harness by himself.

Seals are too smart, too valuable, believes Harry Goodridge, to be wantonly destroyed. They can be taught much—and not only tricks. Right now Harry Goodridge is working with the Navy on a project that will train a seal to detect a diver or equipment underwater, either to pinpoint them for rescuers or to bring them to the surface themselves. Harry's seals have already ferreted out a concealed diver a quarter-mile away in ninety seconds, and have located a diver up to four miles distant, going to him unerringly the moment they are released.

How they do this no one yet knows. It is thought the seal may have a built-in sonar system, perhaps in his whiskers. That whatever it is can be put to practical use is undeniable. Around marine projects, for example—oil rigs, construction jobs, and so on—thousands of dollars' worth of tools are lost annually. Seals can be trained to retrieve them.

Bodies too. Harry tells of his and his son's diving, successfully, for a girl who had drowned in her car in a quarry. "It made me wonder if I could teach Andre to bring up a body. I started working with a big plastic doll. Andre gets it up right away." The only thing delaying the final test—that of Andre's surfacing with a lifesize body—is for Harry to find a plastic manniken, more the size and configuration of an adult human. "They (the mannikens) are all made out of that crumbly stuff that disintegrates."

. . . Depredation of seals by man continues in their immature range, pups being captured for zoos, for wild-animal parks, for biological research and for use as pets. They are also shot for sport and used for target practice.

. . . Depredations of seals by man have been considerable. Normally a friendly animal, the seal has developed a fear of man, establishing its nesting area as far from him as possible and submerging its infants at his approach.

. . . Shooting of seals by lobstermen, at least on the southern Maine coast, appears to be waning, possibly because of protest by conservationists or because evidence suggests that the seal's diet, mostly "trash" fish, does not include the lobster. Shooting of seals by seiners, because of damage by them to the seines, also appears to be on the wane "because there aren't that many seals around."

. . . Seals are extraordinarily intelligent. They can be taught not only tricks but feats useful to man.

. . . Maine law to protect the seal is almost nonexistent. What legislation there is prohibits, in the shooting of seals, the use of weapons dangerous to humans, thus protecting the human rather than the seal. Even this law is in effect only in four small and widely scattered sections of the Maine coast.

. . . Legislation to protect the Maine harbor seal is long overdue.

What is the present state of these beguiling mammals? What has been done to protect them? Will they join the growing number of animals already extinct on our planet? Will they be seen only in museums? Will some child hear from its great-great grandparents of how they had actually *seen* seals frisking in play within sight of onlookers on the shore, or sunning on flat rocks, their fur sleek and shining from salt spray? Is extinction, after all, to be the fate of the seal?

"No, probably not," says Steven Katona, a biologist at the College of the Atlantic in Bar Harbor, Maine. "They've increased since the national Marine Mammal Protection Act went into effect in 1972. It's estimated there are about fifteen thousand harbor seals and three hundred gray seals in the Gulf of Maine now. Both are widespread species." Dr. Katona added, "There are thousands of harbor seals throughout the North Atlantic ocean. They're also found in the North Pacific."

A survey in 1973 by marine biologist David Richardson (deceased) showed a seal population of 5,800. An aerial survey in 1986 by Professor James Gilbert (Wildlife Department, University of Maine) recorded 14,500. The protection act, noted above, may have sent a message to the mother seal that she can now have her baby considerably less threatened by the guns of man. Epidemic diseases also (e.g., distemper) that decimated seals in the past, seem to have diminished.

Our harbor seals, once thought moving toward extinction, are with us yet.

Maine Lobsters

July 26, 1972

GASTRONOMICALLY speaking, it is probably the lobster that brings people to Maine. But these days natives and visitors alike are tightening their belts. Lobster is expensive enough in Maine but in places beyond it has reached the incredible price of twelve dollars or more a pound.

It was not always thus. In colonial days lobster was a "poor man's dish." Early settlers, to fertilize their fields, even plowed them under. To catch lobsters required only a wade into shallow waters where they were ferreted out from under rocks and seaweed.

Read this in a 1605 journal of an exploratory voyage along the coast of Maine: "And toward night we drew with a small net of twenty fathoms very nigh the shore; we got about thirty very good and great lobsters . . . which I omit not to report, because it sheweth how great a profit the fishing would be . . . "

Two hundred years go by and fishermen are hooking lobsters up into their boats with long-handled gaffs. Lobsters sold for a penny apiece in those days, and about as many ended up as bait for cod fishing as were eaten. It wasn't until 1840 that the handwriting on the wall was glimpsed and laws were enacted on the minimum size that could be caught.

Once ten-pound lobsters were common, but catches in the 1870s averaged 2½ to 3 pounds and today's average less than half that size. Recorded in colonial times were lobsters five feet long in New York Bay. Lobsters heavier than forty pounds and with claws that could amputate a human arm have been caught in this century.

But lobsters have grown scarce and fishermen go farther and farther offshore to sink their traps. In these relatively unfished areas lobsters twenty-five pounds and a hundred years old have been hauled into the boats. This is rare though. A female lays an estimated 124,000 eggs a year. About 99 percent serve as food for other lobsters and for fish. Grown, a lobster's weaponry is formidable. Its claws can lay about it a boneyard of marine life. Only when it periodically sheds its shell as it grows, and before a new one forms, is it prey for any passing fish or even another lobster (yes, they are cannibalistic). And, of course, a lobster has not yet developed the intelligence to figure a way out of that trap.

Marine scientists are trying to hit on a safe and economical method to raise lobsters in large quantities. Meanwhile, if you're rich, "bon appétit." If you're not—well, how about mackerel? It may have fed on eggs of lobster or even on the shell-shed lobster. This is as close as the less privileged can get to lobster these days. Happy they who have never developed a taste for it!

Put aside your fears that the Maine lobster is approaching extinction. Because of the large influx of lobster-loving tourists, and because lobsters are shipped from Maine in great quantities throughout the world, it had been thought this succulent crustacean was on its way out.

Marine Patrol Officer Carl Burdin, who operates under the aegis of the Maine Department of Marine Resources, reassures us that since the laws governing lobster trapping changed in 1989, the catch has seemed to remain the same each year. Previously any lobster under $3\frac{3}{16}$ inches had to be returned to the sea; in 1989 this figure was gradually increased to $3\frac{1}{4}$ inches where it has remained.

"Aside from that," says Burdin, "there haven't been many changes in lobstering." Lobstering states are under equal restrictions except, according to Burdin, that Maine is the only one not allowed to trap the oversize lobster. Why? Because for years the large lobster was considered "breed stock," preserved to assure static population. This assumption is questioned by Maine lobstermen. The oversize lobster, they claim, breeds at the time they shed their shells, which is only once in several years. Conversely the small lobsters—those of the size allowed to be trapped—shed two to three times a year, depending on their size. The advantage given to the lobstermen of other states therefore is questioned by their brotherhood in Maine.

Living Off The Land

Undated

GENERAL CECIL MOORE ("Dinty" to his friends) and his wife Esther live in what some say is the oldest house in Arundel (originally a part of Kennebunkport). Behind it are deep woods and a gully that has a small stream winding through it. On two sides of the house are partial woods. It was in one of these, while strolling around his property one day, that Dinty Moore saw three huge white objects glimmering in the bosky dusk.

As a practical engineer, the thought of flying saucers never crossed his mind, and as a general he approached the objects fearlessly. They offered no resistance. He bent over and examined them. Undoubtedly they were mushrooms of some gigantic species unknown to him.

He called mycologist (mushroom expert) G. Warren Cochrane (who, however, claims amateur status). Warren jumped into his car and tore over the road to Arundel. He leaned down, examined the monsters, and straightened up. "Calvatia Cyathiformis," he said in the sonorous tones of those called upon to answer esoteric questions. "They are edible, of superior quality."

Esther Moore describes them thus:

When I cut one in half it was as solid as cream cheese. I cut it in squares and sauteed it and served it as a vegetable. They're much more delicate in taste than the mushrooms I've picked on the Arundel golf course. But they smell pretty mushroomy before they're cooked. One of them I treated according to directions in Stalking the Wild Asparagus. *That's a cookbook I have. Just sauteed it a little and packed it away in the deep freeze. Warren says they are a plant and the puff is the bloom.*

Esther Moore looked them up in an encyclopedia and found that "all of the puff balls with white flesh are good to eat and some of them are very superior to other mushrooms. Found throughout the temperate zone and in some localities they become very abundant after heavy rainfalls." (Caveat: Do not indulge without first making positive identification.)

Who says you can't live off the land in Arundel?

All six characters of this story—Dinty and Esther Moore, Warren Cochrane, and the three mushrooms—have gone to their heavenly rewards. Descendants of the three humans are spread throughout the world. Descendants of the three mushrooms presumably still cling to home ground in Arundel. Will future owners of that property venture forth to "live off the land"—if only to enrich their meals with Calvatia Cyathiformis?

Halloween

Date lost in old files

THEY TELL ME the time may come when I will have almost total recall of my childhood, the time when memory of what happened yesterday is lost but happenings of more than half a century past are crystal clear.

I comfort myself that I'm not old yet, because my childhood is still pretty much of a haze. There is one night, though, that emerges precise and whole whenever I push the memory button. It is the Halloween when I was twelve.

It was my only Halloween, by the way. I stopped being a child before the next one came along and I have no recollection of any before. I lived in cities, and Halloween must have meant only pumpkins and cats and witches drawn at school with crayola, or black and orange candies at Schrafft's. There is no memory at all of walking the city streets in a costume, of ringing doorbells of apartments, or of doors opened by grownups who dispensed candy.

The summer that I was twelve my father died and my mother moved from Boston to Portland to be near her parents. That fall I was placed in the eighth grade of a grammar school in the western part of the city. It was a new life for me. Some may laugh at my calling Portland "country," but to a child whose playground had been first Newark, then Boston streets, whose memory of the walk to school holds no tree nor blade of grass, Portland was to me then what the Mt. Katahdin region of northern Maine is now.

Came October, and with it Halloween, that year when I was twelve. About five eighth graders invited me to join them on a nocturnal prowl. Their goal was the house of a man who "hated children." I recall only two of the group, Harriet Davis and Janice Reed. What became of Harriet I don't know. Janice is now Janice Doherty who writes "Town and Country" for the *Portland Sunday Telegram*. I must ask her sometime if she recalls that Halloween.

We were dressed in sheets, I think. I know we were armed. I remember the piece of soap Harriet gave me. I hadn't the foggiest idea what it was for. The others had to tell me. We headed for the Western Promenade. As we neared our victim's house we took on stealth. I remember vaulting over his low stone wall and creeping up a sloping lawn. The ground beneath my feet felt wonderful – spongy, and slippery with wet leaves. It carried to my nose something foreign to a city child, the smell of earth preparing for its winter sleep, sweet but with a bit of tang. There was a vague whisper in the trees and bushes around us. It was caused by the breeze through the last-clinging leaves, but I preferred to think it was caused by creatures of the night. A delicious feeling of terror tingled my stomach.

The house was in darkness. The Man Who Hated Children must be out. We straightened from our crouching crawl and, emboldened, moved on in ghostly phalanx and reached the house. We each chose a window which was to be a canvas for invective against the MWHC. I grasped my soap firmly in my right hand and raised my arm.

As if it had been a signal, the lights of the house flashed on and caught us, congealed, five little statues of liberty with five raised arms. The front door flew open. Framed in the doorway was THE MAN. "You lousy brats," he yelled. He jerked his head toward someone who fluttered wraith-like behind him. "Mary, go phone the police. I'll hold 'em till they get here." And he started for us.

Here memory fails. I reach for, but cannot grasp, the mental picture of what I did next. I remember very well what Harriet did, though, and I suppose we all did the same. Harriet, fat and short-legged, never touched the ground. Zooming as on a broomstick back to the stone wall, she shot over it like a rocket and headed for home. We could hear "Mary's" voice grow fainter as we built up distance. "John," she was pleading, "Please don't. They're only children. They don't mean any harm."

Were we frightened? You bet. Chastened? I can speak only for myself. Mixed with fright was something else. I'd had, I realized, the time of my life. I think it released something festering, some coltish wish, repressed till then, to kick my heels and raise a bit of hell. In any case, the next year we were thirteen and in high school, and Halloween was put away with other childish things. For me it died without ever having really lived.

Perhaps that is why, since coming to Kennebunk, each year I have bought with something more than indulgence all that stuff, put it on the chest beside my front door, turned on the outside lights and set myself down to await those first scurrying feet up the path, the first giggles, the sudden silence to dredge up courage, and the first ring of the doorbell — which gives me my cue to open the door in terror at the horrible sights confronting me. The pirates and spacemen, the Draculas and King Kongs, the monkeys and rabbits. I have loved best, though, simply the sheets and the children in them, tripping and stumbling, cradling a jack-o'-lantern and clutching the enormous bag that will be tomorrow's stomachache.

Halloween is kid's day. Name any other nationally observed day that is as much so. Christmas and Thanksgiving are shared with grown-ups, and there's not much to Fourth of July any more (to my mind rightly so). There should remain one night when kids take things into their own hands. One night when those awesome creatures called grownups have to bend down and yield up something toothsome or suffer the consequences. One night when grownups are reduced (or appear to be) to a quivering jelly of fright. One night, if you will, of revenge.

I have been lucky with Halloweens as an adult. There's been no soap on my windows because it's inconvenient to get at them past all my bushes. My car is garaged, so no air has been let out of my tires. And it would be gilding the lily to break my broken fences. If these things had happened to me perhaps I would not be this sanguine about Halloween. Others have suffered them. And it was really for them, the sufferers, wasn't it, that the children's party was held Friday night in Kennebunk under police auspices and presumably with parental blessing? "Take the kids off the streets, give them a good time, keep them out of mischief." Kids are adaptable. They probably had a good time. There were prizes, donated by the merchants, and gifts for everybody. There were games. But I think the children would have had a better time roaming the streets, ringing doorbells, irritating the grownups.

Then there is UNICEF, of which I, like nearly everyone, am a strong supporter. On the face of it nothing seems more worthwhile than young people turning the energy spent on greed (all that stuff in their bags) and mischief (soap, tires) toward something charitable like UNICEF. But again it is imposed on the youngsters by us adults. I cannot see any normal small child saying to his mother, "Look, Mom, I want to do something constructive on Halloween for a change. How about if I take a UNICEF carton around this year instead of trick or treat?" I might admire a child like that; I don't think I'd want to see much of him. Collecting for UNICEF is a great cause, but it can be done without sacrificing Halloween to it. Children learn about charity in other ways than by those that take their fun from them.

Let the children have their whispers, their giggles, their furtive scurryings up to strangers' doors. Stop making them feel ashamed that they'd rather stuff their stomachs with loot than hear coins drop into a UNICEF box. Stop giving them parties just so we adults can pursue our evening's activities uninterrupted.

Give Halloween back to them and let them have their one collective night in the moon. It is a short enough night.

Towns' and parents' parties, to eliminate vandalism on this night of nights called Halloween, are well established now. A few parents, or older siblings drafted for the job, still take their toddlers trick-or-treating and often continue on to the parties. Either way you look at it, it's a big night for the kids. Note: smashed pumpkins in the streets, purloined from neighborhood steps, *appear* to be diminishing in late years. This is not a subject that lends itself easily to statistics. By the way, Harriet has gone to that pumpkin in the sky. Janice is perhaps even more alive than on that halcyon night when all of us were twelve.

Index

MAINE
IN TRANSITION

has been published in a first edition
of fifteen hundred copies.
Designed by A. L. Morris,
the text was composed in Paladium
and printed by Knowlton & McLeary
in Farmington, Maine on Champion Pageantry Text.
The jacket was printed on Warren's Offset Enamel Gloss
and the binding in Holliston Mills' Roxite
was executed by New Hampshire Bindery
in Concord, New Hampshire.